AF226208

Quarterly Essay

Quarterly Essay is published four times a year by Black Inc., an imprint of Schwartz Books Pty Ltd. Publisher: Morry Schwartz.

ISBN 9781760642686 ISSN 1832-0953

Subscriptions – 1 year print & digital
(4 issues): $79.95 within Australia incl. GST. Outside Australia $119.95. 2 years print & digital (8 issues): $149.95 within Australia incl. GST. 1 year digital only: $49.95.

Payment may be made by Mastercard or Visa, or by cheque made out to Schwartz Books. Payment includes postage and handling.

To subscribe, fill out and post the subscription card or form inside this issue, or subscribe online:

quarterlyessay.com
subscribe@blackincbooks.com
Phone: 61 3 9486 0288

Correspondence should be addressed to:

The Editor, Quarterly Essay
Level 1, 221 Drummond Street
Carlton VIC 3053 Australia
Phone: 61 3 9486 0288 / Fax: 61 3 9011 6106
Email: quarterlyessay@blackincbooks.com

Editor: Chris Feik. Management: Elisabeth Young. Publicity: Anna Lensky. Design: Guy Mirabella. Assistant Editor: Kirstie Innes-Will. Production Coordinator: Marilyn de Castro. Typesetting: Tristan Main.

For Tom Blaine 1949–2011

"To appear ordinary, just like everybody else, is sometimes a necessary condition for success in Australia. When this is merely a disguise it can frustrate talent but not suppress it; unfortunately, all too often it is not a disguise."

—Donald Horne

"We're victims of our own success."

—Scott Morrison

<table>
<tr><td>

T O P
B L O K E S

</td><td>

The Larrikin Myth,
Class and Power

</td></tr>
</table>

Lech Blaine

WHO WANTS TO BE A BATTLER?

Scott Morrison is the descendant of convicts and the son of a copper. He sympathises with both the swagman and the squatter. In this way, "ScoMo" perfectly encapsulates the identity crisis at the heart of Australia.

"I love Australia," Morrison told the Menzies Research Centre in 2018. "Who loves Australia? Everyone. We all love Australia. Of course we do. But do we love all Australians? That's a different question, isn't it? Do we love all Australians? We've got to … Whether they've become an Australian by birth ten generations ago, when my ancestors came – not by choice, but in chains, rocked up in 1788 – they did alright."

After serving in the army, Scott's old man, John, joined the NSW Police Force and played rugby union for Randwick. Sydney was a city riven with political and religious divisions. The working class even had their own sport: rugby league. In 1908, Irish-Catholic larrikins had protested against the lack of match payments by joining the rival code. Rugby union players from the North Shore and the eastern suburbs were known as "rah-rahs."

Rugby league players from working-class suburbs like Redfern and Balmain were nicknamed "mungos," short for mongrels.

"Rugby league was the bastard child that got away from rugby union," Peter Beattie – the former Labor premier of Queensland – once told me. "It fitted within that whole Ned Kelly psychology of rebellion." The blacksmiths and boilermakers paid to play rugby league were philosophically kindred with bushrangers, trade unions and the Vatican. The stockbrokers and doctors who played rugby union for free were allied with elite private schools, Protestantism and Buckingham Palace.

Scott Morrison was raised on the side of the toffs, not the battlers. His dad, John, and mum, Marion, were salt-of-the-earth Presbyterians, à la Robert Menzies. They belonged to the Liberal Party's moral middle class. The Morrisons popped out two sons – Alan and Scott – before dropping into the newly merged Uniting Church in Bondi Junction. John was the leader of the Boys' Brigade and Marion the leader of the Girls' Brigade. What did the Christian copper's younger son do for fun? He signed up to a theatre group with Mum and Dad and starred in a TV ad for cough drops: "Vicks'll lick a ticklin' throat."

Scott Morrison was an extremely obedient drama kid who played rugby union like his rah-rah father. "Rugby [union] will always be my game," he tweeted in 2012. Yet the two defining themes of Morrison's youth are a precocious puritanism and the blind faith that he comes from humble suburban beginnings. He recalls his childhood as being "run-of-the-mill" and "nothing out of the ordinary." "Bronte was a lot different back then than it is today," Morrison told *The Australian* before the 2017 budget.

The beachside suburb of Bronte might appear second-rate and far away from everything if you've got mates in Double Bay, where Morrison might seem like Darryl Kerrigan compared to Malcolm Turnbull. But Morrison's upbringing was suspiciously close to that of the inner-city elite. He played the saxophone at Sydney Boys High, a selective public school next to the SCG and a member of the prestigious Athletic Association of the Great Public Schools of New South Wales (AAGPS). The AAGPS was an Antipodean outcrop of the British aristocracy. Morrison made the 1st VIII for rowing and 1st XV for rugby union, two leisure activities of the affluent. On bore-watered GPS ovals, "Scotty-Mo" possibly crossed paths with Barnaby Joyce, a sullen boarder across the harbour at Riverview, and James Packer, a cricket fanatic at Cranbrook. "I learned that you don't have to be rolling in money to be happy," Morrison told *The Australian*, "as long as you're all together and helping each other."

The eastern suburbs of Sydney, where Morrison grew up, were arguably the most concentrated pocket of prosperity in one of the world's richest countries. Sydney Boys High might not have been Riverview or Cranbrook. Bronte wasn't Bellevue Hill. Still, it wasn't Blacktown, let alone Broken Hill. By the same token, Scott's father wasn't exactly Kerry Packer. But John Morrison was an extremely well-connected public servant who sat on Waverley Council for two decades. In 1986, John served simultaneously as mayor of Waverley and as a chief inspector of the NSW Police Force. The "modest" house that Morrison's parents inherited from a widowed aunt – where Scotty-Mo stoically shared a bedroom with his older brother, Alan, until high school – sold for $1.5 million in 2001. Morrison felt like a suburban battler relative to the children of multi-millionaires, not realising that his close proximity to this cult of blind privilege was itself a geographical miracle. It is one thing to be lucky, and another to dedicate your life to hoarding luck from those who need some.

At the University of New South Wales, Morrison enrolled in a bachelor of science, followed by an honours degree in economics and geography. The budding everyman of Australian politics completed a highbrow thesis. It was titled: "Religion and Society, a Micro Approach: An Examination of the Christian Brethren Assemblies in the Sydney Metropolitan Area, 1964–1989."

John Morrison didn't let Scott join the Bronte Surf Life Saving Club or attend rock concerts, fearing that he'd succumb to temptations of the flesh and the thirst. "He said the guys in the surf club drank too much and he didn't want me exposed to that," Morrison told *The Australian Women's Weekly*, confessing that he'd been drunk exactly once. Morrison celebrated his twenty-first birthday by marrying childhood sweetheart Jenny. Matchmaker Lynelle played maid-of-honour at the wedding. Jenny had been bridesmaid at Lynelle's own nuptials to a weird unit named Tim Stewart, who would later become nationally famous for spreading QAnon conspiracy theories about how the world is run by cannibalistic paedophiles.

Scott Morrison is a devout wowser. Not even he could invent a character that more egregiously contradicts Australia's self-image as a nation of laid-back larrikins. Morrison's solitary attempt at rebelling against his father was threatening to study theology in Canada after university. So John Morrison – not just your average battler – lined up Scotty a job with the Property Council of Australia. The closest that Morrison came to battling – or being a larrikin, for that matter – was getting cast as the Artful Dodger in *Oliver!*.

"Australian anti-authoritarianism is a big performance," says Melissa Lucashenko. "It's like when you watch *Les Misérables* at the theatre. There are all these upper-middle-class people cheering on the French Revolution, so long as the radicals are actors. Walk outside and if there's a black kid shop-lifting a can of Coke or a packet of smokes, it's the end of the friggin' world."

Lucashenko is a Miles Franklin–winning Indigenous author from Queensland. Her mother was a Bundjalung woman. Her father – an itin-erant Russian migrant – worked at various times as a gold miner, a cane cutter and a meat worker. She describes her dad as a quintessential "lar-rikin," who was also extremely violent. "I knew that we were poor," she says. "I remember Mum scoffing at Dad for wanting bacon and eggs for breakfast. That was for rich people." Lucashenko is just a year older than Morrison, but they had vastly different experiences of Australia's class sys-tem. By the age of seventeen, she was caring for three small children in Eagleby, southwest of Brisbane. According to her 2013 essay "Sinking Below Sight," Eagleby belongs to "the Black Belt": a strip of lower socio-economic suburbs stretching from Ipswich to the tips of the Gold Coast.

"Welfare recipients and the working poor in the Black Belt don't neces-sarily realise they are hard up," Lucashenko wrote for *Griffith Review*, winning a Walkley. "More accurately, many don't realise just how poor they are, since everyone in their lives is battling … I believed that nearly all Australians lived like we did, with far too many animals, dying cars and bugger-all disposable income. In most such families, being rich is the stuff of pure fantasy, and the rare relative (usually distant) who is a business owner or a professional is seen as a beacon of jaw-dropping achievement."

For six years, Morrison worked as a white-collar propagandist for the Property Council. The late bloomer didn't move out of home until the age of twenty-four. In 1995, now twenty-seven, he departed to be deputy CEO of the Australian Tourism Taskforce. It was a fruitful period; he also joined the Liberal Party. That same year, Scott and Jenny bought a unit on Pacific Street in Bronte. They negatively geared it for leverage, and bought a Californian bungalow on Lugar Brae Avenue, two streets from where Morrison grew up. Their second property cost $330,000. The median national house price was $129,800. They sold Lugar Brae Avenue for $985,000 in 2009. Morrison hasn't spoken about when or for how much they sold the Pacific Street unit.

"I remember the first place I bought with Jenny," he said in 2018, neglecting to clarify whether he was talking about his negatively geared investment property or primary address. "It was 53 square metres, it was not very big. It was very, very small. But that was what we could afford, and that's how we made our start."

A year after Morrison joined the Liberal Party, John Howard was elected prime minister. Morrison ruthlessly defected from the Labor-friendly Australian Tourism Taskforce to the rival Tourism Council, operated by Bruce Baird, former state Liberal minister and father of future NSW premier Mike Baird. Two years later, Bruce – a fellow Christian – was elected federal member for Cook. His protégé Morrison moved to New Zealand, accepting a newly invented position as director of the Office of Tourism and Sport.

The rah-rah described the rugby union–mad nation as "a bit of a nirvana – in Sydney, rugby usually takes second place to league."

But the adopted homeland didn't quite reciprocate his affection. Kiwi journalist Nick Venter described the Aussie spin-doctor as "like a cross between Rasputin and Crocodile Dundee ... Here he is, whispering into the minister's ear about the board. There he is, crashing through the undergrowth without regard for reputation or bureaucratic convention."

Within two years, Morrison was sent packing in acrimonious circumstances. Back home, patron Bruce Baird tipped him off about a vacancy for the director of the NSW Liberal Party. At the age of thirty-two, a political greenhorn snagged the high-profile position. Meanwhile, Jenny Morrison added a $325,000 holiday home in the Blue Mountains to the couple's property portfolio. Scott failed to win any state elections during a four-year term, but he did contribute to Howard's back-to-back federal victories.

In 2004, Joe Hockey promoted Morrison to be the CEO of Tourism Australia on $350,000 a year. The Bronte battler's salary was higher than the PM's, and approximately seven times the national average. Morrison oversaw the disastrous "So where the bloody hell are you?" campaign, featuring Lara Bingle, while igniting a civil war with tourism minister Fran Bailey. Then he was sacked in roughly the same time frame as the hapless stint in New Zealand. He reportedly received a $500,000 golden handshake.

Donald Horne had never been more on the money: "Australia is a lucky country run by second-rate people who share its luck."

Scott Morrison rocketed to the top of a mock meritocracy populated by mediocre GPS boys, who scratched each other's backs until there wasn't any skin or fingernails left. "I'm a mortgage-belt Liberal," he told Triple M in 2018. "I've got a mortgage like everyone else. I've got two young kids, nine and eleven, going to school. That's the centre of my life, is my family. The values that come out of being a dad, the values that come out of just living a life in the suburbs of Sydney."

Call it the politics of envy. But I don't reckon the average suburbanite is lucky enough to live a few minutes from the beach — and twenty minutes from the Sydney CBD — while attending a selective school and then one of the best universities in the country, before their influential dad scores them a well-paid job as a lobbyist for the real estate industry. Nor do most battlers live at home while saving up for property deposits, or prosper from a six-figure payout after getting sacked for being bad at their job. It ain't exactly the stuff of struggle Slim Dusty or Jimmy Barnes sing about.

According to Robert Menzies, Morrison deserves the social and economic advantages provided by geography, education and nepotism: "To say the industrious and intelligent son of self-sacrificing and saving and forward-looking parents has the same social deserts and even material needs as the dull offspring of stupid and improvident parents is absurd." The short shrift: eat shit, serfs! This moral justification for poverty is a central pillar of Morrison's political beliefs and Pentecostalism. The problem is that it deeply contradicts Australia's self-mythology about being a bastion of the fair go. So Scott John Morrison – a tall poppy from the eastern suburbs – needed to reinvent himself as ScoMo, a top bloke from the Sutherland Shire who loves rugby league. In doing so, he plagiarised the nickname and personal hobby of Anthony "Albo" Albanese.

Albanese – now federal Labor leader – was a working-class larrikin from central casting. His mother was Irish-Catholic. She met Carlo Albanese on an ocean liner from Sydney to England. He was an Italian ship steward engaged to a woman back home. Anthony was conceived on the high seas and raised in public housing by a single mum on the disability pension. He was the living and breathing personification of all the classist stereotypes about rugby league fans being bogans, bludgers and bastards. "I was raised with three great faiths: the Labor Party, the Catholic Church and the South Sydney Rabbitohs," said Albanese, giving me his routine stump speech.

Anthony Albanese is a life member of the Rabbitohs. Scott Morrison's ScoMo persona was a focus-grouped act of identity theft. The success of Boris Johnson's Brexit and the election of Donald Trump demonstrated a longing for leaders who didn't look or sound like career politicians. So Albo the self-deprecating stats nerd became ScoMo the ocker jock. It was the perfect crime. Most of the general public didn't know ScoMo or Albo from a bar of soap. The child actor delivered the replica identity with more chutzpah, but none of the empathy that comes from being an actual outsider.

"Morrison doesn't even *like* rugby league," Albanese protests to me. "Before he was the member for Cook, rugby league didn't get a mention. He's a rugby union guy from the eastern suburbs … He wouldn't have a clue."

Why would a career politician camouflage as working-class? For power. Australia is divided between cosmopolitans and parochials. The cosmopolitans – well educated and affluent – are concentrated in Sydney, Canberra and Melbourne. Cosmopolitans from the left and right dominate the media and political classes. Many are small-l Liberals. The heartland for the Liberal Party – and rugby union – is the North Shore and the eastern suburbs of Sydney: the seats of North Sydney, Warringah, Bradfield, Mackellar, Berowra and Wentworth. Since Federation, none of them has elected a Labor candidate.

But prime ministers are elected by parochials: aka Quiet Australians, or bogans. Parochials are located on the fringes of cities and in the regions. They are far less likely to have a university degree. And a whole heap of them are in the decentralised convict states of New South Wales and Queensland, where rugby league has been the main winter passion of the proletariat since 1908. John Fahey – the former Liberal premier of New South Wales and a finance minister in the Howard government – watched many on the left develop an anaphylactic reaction to working-class culture post-Whitlam. "I saw a number of things suggesting [that] Labor Party people in Sydney found hobnobbing with captains of industry at rugby union test matches to be better than a pie and a beer at a suburban rugby league game," Fahey told me shortly before his death in 2020.

It wasn't just conservatives who picked up the class cringe. Megan Davis – a proud Cobble Cobble woman from regional Queensland – holds the Balnaves Chair in Constitutional Law and is pro vice-chancellor at UNSW. She grew up in Eagleby. After moving to Sydney and rising through the ranks of academia, Davis noticed urban progressives were allergic to the c-word, and oblivious to her lived experience of poverty. When Davis mentioned the economic hardship of her upbringing, privileged sympathisers insisted that their parents knew what it was like to battle too. "My family was the underclass," she says. "Our place in Eagleby was like any tiny housing commission home. Worn-out furniture. No floor coverings. Heaps of siblings. Lots of noise. We had to eat porridge biscuits leading up to pay day because there was no food left … The middle class of Sydney don't know what it looks like to be poor, because poor people are so hidden here."

Davis is now a commissioner of the Australian Rugby League. She is a diehard rugby league fan, making her something of a rarity among the upper echelons of academia. She consistently hears Australia's academic and media elite register disdain for working-class people – such as her family – via a socially acceptable loathing for rugby league. "Class is the last taboo," Davis told me in 2020. "Clever progressives buy into so many negative tropes about poor and uneducated people. And they would do it to no other group of marginalised people."

John Howard understood that the art of realpolitik required converting traditional enemies, not shouting louder at the North Shore. So he expertly deployed the symbols, values and vernacular of working-class culture to attract jilted battlers from Labor's blue-collar base, creating a fresh electoral map for the Liberals. In 1996, the Coalition won twenty-nine seats from Labor. Twenty-one of them were in outer-suburban, regional or rural New South Wales and Queensland. That made the archetypal Howard Battler a rugby league fan without a university degree. They leaned to the left on economic issues and the right on social ones.

My foster brother John is a dyed-in-the-wool Howard Battler. John comes from the underclass. In 1985, his biological parents were sent to Boggo Road Gaol for kidnapping, and for stalking Joh Bjelke-Petersen. John was eighteen months old and grossly underweight. The prison guards believed his mum was at risk of committing infanticide. John was placed into foster care with my parents in Rosedale, a one-pub town on the outskirts of Bundaberg. His stint in Boggo Road was the only time that he's ever lived in an urban area.

"I can be in a crowd of so-called *well-to-do* people," says John, "who consider themselves to be above the working class. But it gets very draining, mate."

John inherited bipolar II from his biological mother. University was never for him. He became an unskilled labourer, before working as a bartender at my father's pubs. John beat all of the obstacles in his life to become a successful car salesman and a loving father, breaking a cycle of poverty and child abuse. He remains viscerally aware that Australia is split between the haves and the have-nots. One of his biological brothers died of a heroin overdose after a decade in and out of jail. But unlike our dad's generation of Labor-voting larrikins, John's vivid lived experience of Australia's class system inspires him to vote for the Liberals.

"I identified with a particular leader," he tells me. "Which was John Howard. Stoic sort of bloke. Not a big talker. But said just enough. And for a nerdy guy with glasses, he didn't shy away from a fight. Like with the gun lobby. Or the GST. You respect a little bloke like that for having a go."

Under Menzies, the Liberal Party turned class into a taboo subject. Howard weaponised the elephant in the corner of Australian society. By fleecing parochials from Labor, he turned them into the kingmakers of Australian politics. But Howard was easily distinguishable from his battlers by the brand of tracksuit he wore on morning walks around Kirribilli: rugby union's Australian Wallabies, not a suburban rugby league team.

"John Howard went into the dressing rooms after the grand final to have a beer, and looked like a complete dork," says a former cabinet colleague of Scott Morrison. "But people appreciated that. He wasn't trying to be something that he's not. Whereas Morrison does try to be something that he's not. Scotty from Marketing, as his critics call him."

In 2019, Morrison won an unwinnable election by pretending to *be* a Howard Battler. By drinking a beer at Shark Park on a Sunday arvo, ScoMo superimposed himself into rugby league's rich history of egalitarianism. He was communicating a clear-cut message to NRL fans in the marginal seats of New South Wales and Queensland: *I respect you*. Better yet, his NRL fandom – and blokey aphorisms – provoked mockery from snobs in the inner city, making him even more likeable within the hushed-up suburbs and country towns.

"I believe in a fair go for those who have a go in this country," Morrison told the Menzies Research Centre in 2019. "I think that's what fairness means … Remember, my value is: we look after our mates."

My brother John is a larger-than-life larrikin strongly hostile towards authority. He once represented himself in court while fighting a $66 parking fine, and won. His partner didn't finish high school, and works in hospitality. Their three kids go to Bundaberg State High. John played rugby league from the age of five until thirty-five. He routinely spends his Saturday afternoons doing odd jobs around the house, before smashing a six-pack of XXXX Gold while watching the NRL. And Scott Morrison is hands down his favourite prime minister since John Howard. "ScoMo doesn't talk like a toff," says John. "And he seems like a bloke who'd stick up for his mates and his family if push came to shove."

John detects contempt from Australia's media and political classes. He clapped and cheered as ScoMo bashed the "the Canberra Bubble." The PM never referred to himself as working class, or as a battler, or as a larrikin. But a picture is worth a thousand words. And the catchphrases delivered with an ocker accent were indisputable. He was a pastiche of John Howard and Paul Hogan. "ScoMo is as larrikin as you can get," says John. "He goes to the footy and loves a beer like everyone else." The Sharks-loving, beer-drinking, Bunnings-visiting shtick was a slick manoeuvre to kindle a quick intimacy with legitimate battlers, who might otherwise be suspicious of his ambitiousness and puritanism.

You might be thinking: *No shit, Sherlock.* All politicians are frauds. Some are better at pretending to be normal than others. The fascinating thing about the ScoMo hoax is how much it reveals about the delusions of Australia's larrikin tradition, and the way that it betrays the working-class target audience for the Coalition's Culture and Climate Wars.

On 26 January 1788, Morrison's fifth-great-grandfather William Roberts arrived at Sydney Cove, after pinching five and a half pounds of yarn. Roberts married a kindred criminal named Kezia Brown, who arrived lice-infested on the Second Fleet. Scott Morrison wishes that bitter Aboriginal people would stop living in the past and walk a mile in his ancestors' shackles. "You know, when those twelve ships turned up in Sydney, it wasn't a particularly flash day for the people on those vessels either," he said at a press conference in 2021, responding to conjecture about Australia Day.

Five generations later, middle-class Australians like Morrison were no longer ashamed of their convict stain. Criminal kin were a source of authenticity. More importantly, they provided a moral alibi for genocide. *Not all whites*, Morrison was basically saying.

"Among the sports of the military officers and landed gentry, was hunting the blacks," wrote Mary Gilmore, the socialist poet on the $10 note and Scott Morrison's unlikely great-great-auntie. "Grandmother told me that they went out after them with packs of dogs just as they hunted foxes in Ireland ... when it was all over they made a feast and had a ball." Gilmore's grandparents were apparently harassed for objecting to the calculated slaughter. In 1788, there were approximately 750,000 Aboriginal people in Australia. By Federation in 1901, the Aboriginal population was fewer than 100,000. The social isolation of the bush bred a special intensity in the friendships among men, as did the widespread racial cleansing.

"This idea of mateship," says Melissa Lucashenko. "Much of that was about covering up massacres and being implicit in genocide together. You'd want to be very sure that your white mates weren't going to reveal what had gone on the night before, when you went out to shoot blacks together."

This systematic guilt helped shape a mask of ignorance. Playing dumb became second nature. It is comforting to pretend we all accidentally stumbled to the end of the earth and somehow grew rich from pure luck, a bunch of criminals making the best of a crook situation. So please don't ask any hard questions. What the bloody hell would we know?

"Much energy is wasted in pretending to be stupid," wrote Horne.

The innocent victimhood of the convict laid the groundwork for the larrikin, whose incuriousness to the past and future became a moral virtue. In the beginning, larrikins sinned on the streets of Australian cities. They lusted not after power but for moral condemnation from coppers. The capitalist class was trolled for sport. That didn't mean the larrikin was impervious to the seductions of money and media spectacle. Life revolved around get-rich-quick schemes and dreams of widespread notoriety. "The term 'larrikin' was used as a handy way for journalists and the authorities to label any apparently lowborn young person who ... engaged in uncouth behavior," wrote Melissa Bellanta in *Larrikins: A History*. "At all times larrikinism had a profound connection to unskilled labour."

In Sydney, the larrikin was often drawn from Irish-Catholic convict stock, but not exclusively. Many were English battlers emboldened by how dramatically they outnumbered the aristocrats down under. Economic inequality unleashed a plague of working-class rage sublimated into a charade of playfulness. Underneath the gambling, drinking, fighting and petty crime was run-of-the-mill nihilism. Curiously, the larrikin was equally prevalent in Melbourne, which didn't have the same convict stain as Sydney. This indicates that the larrikin was possibly fuelled more by testosterone than a political ideology.

"The larrikins were often found to be the children of respectable parents and in work," wrote historian John Hirst in *The Monthly*. "It was not the defiance of the damaged and excluded; it was the boldness that came from self-confidence, of young men who would not be confined."

It was all fun and games until a spate of gang rapes and racially motivated riots. Ned Kelly – the son of a convict – gave the underclass someone to rally behind. He was born in the same year as the Eureka Stockade, when Irish-Catholic Peter Lalor led an insurrection against the British Empire. Kelly was activated into a full-blown Irish-Catholic terrorist by the wrongful arrest of his mum. His gang of mates assassinated three coppers, derailed a train and took a pub hostage. In a DIY suit of armour, Ned Kelly rode a horse into a barrage of bullets. He survived. "Such is life," uttered drop-dead Ned to the unflinching executioner.

By dying at the age of twenty-five, Kelly became Australia's most famous historical figure. Martin Flanagan has likened Ned to Jesus Christ. Peter Carey called him Australia's Thomas Jefferson, our founding father. "Ned Kelly was an Australian legend," states an official Victorian tourism website aimed at luring grey nomads to the goldfields. "He epitomised many qualities that ordinary Australians admire. He was a larrikin, loyal to his family and ready to sacrifice himself for his mates. An underdog, he represented the struggling classes and thumbed his nose at the establishment."

In 1891, the spirits of Peter Lalor and Ned Kelly guided 3000 striking sheep shearers who marched from Barcaldine to Longreach, thereby starting the Australian Labor Party. Banjo Paterson wrote "Waltzing Matilda" drawing on the plight of striking shearers in rural Queensland. Our fairytale of egalitarianism was immortalised by a solicitor who went to Sydney Grammar.

"The big stories then were of the class struggle, of 'Opening up the land', and of the Empire," wrote Melissa Lucashenko. "It should go without saying that these were stories not only of conquest and bravery, but also of exclusion – sexism and gross racism and homophobia, to name just three."

Banjo Paterson and Henry Lawson competed to be seen as Australia's Nobel laureate of the mate. This literary pissing contest produced a fantastical version of Australian manhood. Despite the presence of Aboriginals, women and migrants at the sites of democratic struggle, larrikinism became seen almost exclusively as the domain of a straight, white, working-class bloke. He was a reckless collectivist desperate for male affection.

"The Australian bushman is born with a mate who sticks to him through life – like a mole," wrote Lawson in "That Pretty Girl in the Army." "A bushman has always a mate to comfort him and argue with him, and work and tramp and drink with him … to lie to the girl for him if he's single, and to his wife if he's married … and each believes that the other is the straightest chap that ever lived – 'a white man!'"

Paterson was overcompensating for affluence. Lawson was overcompensating for effeminacy; he also had a failed relationship with Mary Gilmore. According to Frank Moorhouse in *The Drover's Wife*, Lawson was "passing" as a larrikin. The bard of the bush felt deeply uncomfortable in the company of the shearers and drovers, about whom he waxed lyrical. He was embarrassed by the skinny width of his wrists, so had artists enlarge them in paintings, and grew a cartoonishly long moustache. Moorhouse speculated about the sexual longing between Lawson and Jim Gordon, his best friend. He wouldn't have been the only larrikin repenting for the sin of homosexuality by simulating a rigid virility.

Mateship became the gospel of a federated colony. Once, the larrikin had been an unskilled labourer roaming the streets of the inner city. Trade unions gave untameable mavericks a blue collar and a living wage. The Labor Party provided political self-determination. The church offered a spiritual superannuation scheme and forgiveness for myriad depravities.

At Federation, Australian women became the most fully enfranchised in the world. World War I overshadowed those democratic achievements. Stella award–winning historian Clare Wright believes that Vida Goldstein and Miles Franklin were fair-dinkum larrikins. But the bloodshed at Gallipoli ensured national identity remained tied to imperialism and the bravery of white men. "Gallipoli – with its militarist narrative of youthful sacrifice, not youthful optimism – was not the birth of the nation," wrote Wright in *You Daughters of Freedom*. "It was the death of the nation we were well on the way to becoming."

*

My pop John was nicknamed "Hoppy" due to the limp from a workplace accident. He was a blacksmith on the Ipswich railway and vice-president of the Queensland Ironworkers' Union. During World War II, 3000 people were employed at his workshop, making it the largest job provider in the state. Ipswich – half an hour west of Brisbane – was an old coalmining town with a chip on its shoulder about class, and a fear of recession seared into its soul. Coalmining employed 3000 people. Another couple of thousand worked at the flourishing wool mills.

"The men … reckon they get what Australians call a fair go," explained the narrator of *The New Ipswich*, a quaint documentary released in 1947. "They work a five-day week; get holiday leave with full pay; compensation for injury at work; pensions at retiring age. They work with a sense of security, the most important step on the road to happiness."

My grandmother Lillian was perpetually pregnant. She gave birth sixteen times in the space of twenty-four years. Four of her children died promptly on arrival. Poor Hazel was boiled alive by a saucepan of fat drippings at the age of five. This left my father, Thomas, as the unintended youngest son of eleven siblings. He was born in October 1949. Dad arrived at a sliding-doors moment. The working class enjoyed a false sense of security. Roughly two-thirds of Australia's workforce were members of a trade union. The Irish-Catholic proletariat had a peculiar amount of power, symbolic and concrete.

The previous prime minister, John Curtin, was a Grade Eight dropout from country Victoria. He was succeeded by fellow dropout Ben Chifley, son of a Bathurst blacksmith. Akin to Chifley, Queensland premier Ned Hanlon was a railway worker and trade unionist. Curtin, Chifley and Hanlon were of Irish-Catholic descent, à la Ned Kelly. But they sought economic equality with bills rather than bullets.

"Chifley drove trains, mate!" my father would boast to me.

Chifley – it must be noted – was also an unreconstructed racist. He was elected to parliament after claiming that the conservative government had "allowed so many dagoes and aliens into Australia that today they are all over the country taking work which rightly belongs to all Australians." Robert Menzies was a Scottish Presbyterian with a university degree. He was determined to preserve parliament as a playground for his rival cabal of white blokes. In 1942, while Curtin waged literal war in Papua, Menzies bravely declared rhetorical war in a series of radio broadcasts called "Forgotten People," a shy title for an ex–prime minister with his own radio program.

"Quite recently," said Menzies, "a bishop wrote a letter to a great daily newspaper … His belief, apparently, was that the workers are those who work with their hands. He sought to divide the people of Australia into classes … In a country like Australia the class war must always be a false war."

Menzies was a master of gaslighting working-class people. He called them sooks for noticing the vast discrepancy in living standards and life expectancy between semi-illiterate blacksmiths from Ipswich and university-educated barristers in Kooyong. He demanded a class-war ceasefire. In the very next breath, he re-declared class war on behalf of the calm and affluent. "But if we are to talk of classes," continued Mr Menzies, "then the time has come to say something of the forgotten class – the middle class … who, properly regarded, represent the backbone of this country." Ming the Merciless was talking about a truce rather than a revolution. In the short term, he attempted to stem the flow of power and capital from the aristocracy to the proletariat by awakening the fat voting bloc that sat between them – aka the Forgotten People. Menzies remembered them, and won a landslide victory against Chifley two months after my father's birth.

Not astonishingly, class persisted. My father was the only member of his family who made it past primary school. My nan died of a stroke in 1962. Dad dropped out after Grade Eight. In 1963, he got a job at the Ipswich abattoirs. In 1966, he slipped on the blood and guts of cut-up cattle and fell a metre onto concrete, shattering his hip. He spent six months in hospital with an infection. My pop suffered kidney failure a month before his son's emancipation. Dad walked with a limp for the rest of his life.

The local Labor MP for the federal seat of Oxley was an ex-copper named Bill Hayden. His father had been an Irish-Catholic seaman from California, who illegally abandoned ship in Australia. After the death of his father, a fifteen-year-old Hayden dropped out of school to financially support his mother. "[I] still frequently describe myself as boots and braces working class," said Hayden in 2009. "I've got nothing against the middle class … [But] there are some people in the middle class who seemed to latch onto the Labor Party for their own ends and promotion."

Bill Hayden wasn't blind to the chauvinism within the mate-dominated labour movement. In 1971, at a party conference on the Gold Coast, Hayden moved two motions: to ban boxing and to decriminalise homosexuality. The state president of the Labor Party was a burly boilermaker named Jack Emberton.

"Jesus Christ," Emberton said to Hayden. "I can't follow you. This morning you wanted a law to prevent a man giving another man a manly punch in the nose. And this afternoon you want a law passed to allow poofters to punch a man in the bum. All right. Poofters to the right. Noes to the left."

The labour movement isn't a lost utopia of virtue. Corruption was rife within unions, and prejudices common among the membership. But without the underpinning of class, left-wing politics will remain little more than a virtuous rendition of individualism. Clare Wright warns against "throwing out the baby with the cultural bathwater." She doesn't believe Labor can consistently win federal government until it tells a coherent story that links back to deeper myths about Australian identity. The trick, she believes, is to fill the silences within those myths, rather than disregarding them altogether.

"We don't have to cancel the larrikin," she argues. "We can still embrace them. But it will be a much more interesting story when it's based on evidence and not bullshit … That's why conservatives have been so successful. They've managed to capture that figure and comforted a lot of people, by saying that we don't have to start from scratch in terms of understanding who we are."

John Willey was a real larrikin. When he was six, his mother was admitted to Wolston Park Mental Asylum with post-natal depression. His father buggered off, so John grew up in an orphanage. A primary school dropout and timber cutter from Ipswich, he enlisted and fought in the Battle of Balikpapan, during the last gasps of World War II. When John got back, he didn't attend Anzac Day parades or speak ill of the Japanese. He was a devout republican. It irritated him immensely when monarchists invoked dead diggers to defend the Union Jack's occupation of the Australian flag.

"Soldiers don't die for a flag," he said. "They die trying to stay alive."

John got back to Brisbane in 1946. There was no welcoming party at the wharves. A paper shuffler allocated John to the Ipswich coalmines. He moved home and met Ivy. Bruce was their fourth child of five, and one of my dad's best mates. My parents met in John and Ivy's backyard at a barbeque.

"Dad didn't own a car until he was sixty-odd," says Bruce. "He was up at 3 a.m. Walked to the mine. One of the blokes in a blue singlet with a pick. Covered in black shit. Had a shower after work. Walked to the pub. Home for dinner. Five kids in a three-bedroom cottage. That was a working-class life."

John was a member of the Miners Union. Ivy was the president of the Women's Mining Auxiliary. Along with my father's family, they helped build Railways Rugby League Club, a working-class team in a working-class code. Most of the players were railway workers or coalminers. Three of my aunties met and married unionised footballers. My uncle George was the fullback for the last Ipswich team to win the Bulimba Cup. My first cousin Allan Langer is one of the greatest rugby league players of all time.

Bruce went to Bremer State High, excelling at mathematics. He sat the exam for a Commonwealth Bank cadetship at the end of Grade Ten. Unbeknown to Bruce, his father ripped up the acceptance letter. "No child of mine was getting a job at a bank," he confessed thirty years later.

At the same time, John forbade any of his children from becoming coalminers, owing to the prevalence of black lung and fatal workplace accidents. Three of his sons ended up in the army. He considered the Vietnam War less treacherous than coalmining. Bruce joined the railway as an apprentice electrician. There were 160 apprentices in his intake.

"People weren't rich," says Bruce. "But everyone had a job."

The working class enjoyed secure employment and a tightknit culture, but their political arm was playing up like a second-hand lawn mower. Labor was in the process of losing nine consecutive elections. They were led to three defeats by Arthur Calwell, an Irish-Catholic and White Australia nativist. "I am proud of my white skin, just as a Chinese is proud of his yellow skin, a Japanese of his brown skin, and the Indians of their various hues from black to coffee-coloured," Calwell wrote in his memoir *Be Just and Fear Not*. "Anybody who is not proud of his race is not a man at all."

Phillip Adams was one of the spin doctors tasked with selling Calwell to the masses. After surviving a penniless and abusive childhood, Adams got a job in advertising and joined the Communist Party. This was in the midst of Menzies' scare campaign. Adams split up with communism and started a less revolutionary romance with the Labor Party. "I wandered around working-class shopping centres doing vox pops about Arthur," Adams tells me. "People would shrink away in embarrassment. One said, 'He wears yellow socks with a blue suit!' Another one said, 'He wouldn't know how to use a knife and fork at Buckingham Palace!' There was not so much a cultural cringe as a class cringe towards one of their own."

In 1966, Arthur survived an assassination attempt that was just as lacklustre as his leadership. That year, he lost to Harold Holt in a landslide, before being replaced by Gough Whitlam. On the surface, the ascension of Whitlam – a Presbyterian – was a terrible betrayal of Labor's blue-collar, Irish-Catholic base. He was born at home in Menzies' electorate of Kooyong, the son of a solicitor turned public servant. Gough attended Knox Grammar and Canberra Grammar, before doing an arts degree at the University of Sydney.

"In those days I wasn't real sure about Gough," Bill Hayden admitted decades later. "You know? My working-class prejudices. He was very well suited and he looked different and he sounded different."

The year 1972 was bittersweet for Ipswich. One pitch-black winter morning, Bruce was woken up by a bang, followed by an earthquake. "That's Box Flat," said John, referring to the coalmine that he was due to plunge back into. Seventeen men were killed by an eruption of gas and coal dust, including three of Bruce and my dad's mates at Railways Rugby League Club. Their tortured bodies were never recovered from the scorched earth. Ivy made sandwiches for hysterical widows. John went back to work.

"It's something you never forget," says Bruce.

Bruce turned seventeen in October. He wanted to stay that age forever. The conservatives kept conscripting his teammates to fight the Viet Cong. Bruce's brother enlisted. Fresh from visiting Mao Zedong, Whitlam pledged to end Australia's involvement in the Vietnam War and let the kids of coalminers attend university like he had. He paid a visit to a grief-stricken Ipswich. Bruce wore an "It's Time" shirt to St Paul's, where he handed out how-to-vote cards at the election in a pair of pluggers. He speaks about meeting Whitlam with the intensity of someone reminiscing about first love.

"I don't give a shit if you're Mick Jagger or the Queen of England," says Bruce. "I ain't bowing to no bastard. But I was in awe of Gough as a young fella. He was deadset the only person that I've ever met who made me nervous. What the fuck do you say to Whitlam? I just about wet myself."

Whitlam vowed to deliver universal education and health care to blue-collar battlers. It didn't matter that he was a pacifist and aristocrat who'd visited communist China. Or that he was promising to fully abolish the White Australia policy and acknowledge Indigenous land rights. Or that he was passionately apathetic about rugby league. True-blue communities united behind him because he offered tangible advantages with a massive dash of charisma. Their ultimate solidarity was to class, not culture.

"There's been a rich history of Labor Party leaders – such as Gough Whitlam and Don Dunstan – who had none of the cultural mannerisms of the working class, but who did very, very well indeed," says Phillip Adams.

Bruce's equivalent of Schoolies Week was the 1972 election. It was the first Saturday of December. Labor had been out of power since 1949. It won

49.59 per cent of the national primary vote. In the Central Queensland coalmining electorates of Capricornia and Dawson, Labor received a primary vote of 55.8 per cent and 57.7 per cent. In Pauline Hanson's future electorate of Oxley, Bill Hayden got 65.8 per cent.

"Ipswich hit the piss for a week, I reckon," says Bruce. "My team had copped floggings for twenty-three years. It was like winning the World Cup."

*

1972 was a thrilling but ultimately false dawn for battlers like Bruce, not least because Gough's cabinet was populated by snake oil salesmen. Working-class communities in Queensland and New South Wales had been underpinned by four pillars: the Catholic Church, the Labor Party, trade unions and rugby league. Together, they provided battlers with improvements to living standards, along with social cohesion, self-esteem and the safety net of eternal life. But by the 1970s, those four bastions of blue-collar solidarity were atrophying.

John Fahey's parents were Irish-Catholic immigrants. In 1956, they moved to Picton, a humble township on the western fringe of Sydney. A year earlier, the Catholic Church went through an ugly divorce with the Labor Party in Victoria. The creation of the Democratic Labour Party kept Labor out of power until Gough, and meant that it no longer had sole custody of Irish-Catholics. Menzies inflamed the situation by funnelling money to Catholic schools. Many of their graduates defected to the Liberal Party.

"Once upon a time, working-class families in Western Sydney never came near the Libs," Fahey told me. "I think the first time my father voted Liberal was when I became a candidate."

Fahey was inspired to join the Liberal Party by the election of Whitlam, a Presbyterian from the same patrician mould as Menzies. Fahey noticed the outflux of "down-to-earth" Irish-Catholics from Labor had overlapped with the influx of socially progressive "snobs" from elite private schools and sandstone universities. Call them Gough's Aristocrats.

Meanwhile, the Establishment stumbled upon the untapped cultural and economic capital of passing as working-class. Kerry Packer was the son of a right-wing media tycoon. Kerry boarded at Geelong Grammar, where he played Aussie Rules, cricket, tennis and polocrosse. His maternal grandfather, Herbert, was a doctor who played rugby union for Scotland. There was zero trace of rugby league fanaticism in the Packer family DNA. But in the early 1970s, Kerry got back fat from a business trip to America. So he hired a roughneck rugby league player named John Quayle as his personal trainer.

"I took Kerry Packer to his first Souths game at Redfern Oval," Quayle once told me. "His schooling was Melbourne . . . But he arrives at Redfern in a tracksuit and a terry towelling hat! We had a pie, and he loved it."

Decades later, Australia's richest man still insisted on being served humble pies by compliant butlers at ritzy business lunches. Kerry Packer was Sydney's savviest class crossdresser. He could afford to gamble more on a single game of rugby league than the part-time players earnt in a year from their blue-collar jobs. But the boy born with a silver spoon in his mouth slipped into a tracksuit and reinvented himself.

"Kerry thought of himself as a larrikin," says Philip Adams.

Adams was instrumental in the creation of another fabricated larrikin. He produced *The Adventures of Barry McKenzie*, the first Australian film to exceed a million dollars in box office receipts. Barry McKenzie was the yobbo alter ego of snobby satirist Barry Humphries, most famous for inventing Dame Edna. Humphries grew up comfortable in Menzies' electorate of Kooyong. At Melbourne Grammar, he ignored sport and blitzed the humanities, before studying philosophy and Dadaism at Melbourne University.

"Barry Humphries created larrikin characters," says Adams. "But they were acts of exorcism, because he despised them all."

The runaway success of *Barry McKenzie* triggered a social experiment that highlighted a subtle shift of tone within politics. Adams took Humphries to a shindig at Old Parliament House. A conga line of blue-blooded Liberals sidled up to do their most ocker imitation of Barry McKenzie. By contrast, working-class Labor MPs impersonated the urbane Barry Humphries.

"The Libs affected a faux-mateship – or faux-larrikinism – in their social interactions," Adams tells me. "Whereas there were quite a few Labor Party people who seemed to be trying to escape the gravitational pull of class."

The right-wing larrikin was a social manifestation of what John Hirst called Australia's "democracy of manners." In England, London aristocrats didn't mimic Wigan coalminers. In Australia, everyone was a winner. Imitation was the sincerest form of flattery that privilege could pay to poverty. "Australians blot out differences when people meet face-to-face," wrote Hirst. "They talk to each other as if they are equals."

But Australia was much more comfortable prosecuting the so-called politics of envy in the 1970s than in the new millennium. Roy Masters – the eldest son of acclaimed novelist Olga Masters and brother of journalist Chris Masters – is Sydney's patron saint of class warfare. In 1978, Roy became the Shakespeare-quoting coach of the Western Suburbs Magpies. Masters had a degree in economics. Borrowing from Marx and Freud, the coach nicknamed his team "the Fibros," based on the material used to build the council houses he passed on the way from Penrith to training. He nicknamed rival North Shore glamour team the Manly Sea Eagles "the Silvertails," a phrase plagiarised from a Frank Hardy novel.

"I want you to show two million people out there rugby league was born in the western suburbs, not on the beaches," he said in a motivational speech, according to a 1978 Fairfax profile. Masters tapped into Australia's insider–outsider psychology and sparked a series of violent encounters between the high-flying Sea Eagles and the embattled Magpies.

Australia's most famous fibro was Paul Hogan. "Hoges" grew up in a Granville council house, near the Magpies' home ground at Lidcombe Oval. A blue-collar rigger on the Sydney Harbour Bridge, he rose to prominence by pretending to be a bushman from Lightning Ridge on Channel Nine's *New Faces*. Hoges replicated the premise of *The Adventures of Barry McKenzie*, with much more sincerity. He wasn't taking the mickey out of top blokes. He sanctified them, while cutting down the tall poppies – university-educated intellectuals and feminists – who criticised political incorrectness.

Hogan was a larrikin for hire. He starred in TV ads for Winfield and Foster's Lager, and created *The Paul Hogan Show* for Packer. The show provided an emotional release valve to fibros, without doing anything to improve their standards of living or identify the causes of economic inequality: silvertails like Packer. By loving Hoges so much, the audience destroyed his ordinariness. He was the original cashed-up bogan. "Last time I filled out my tax I remember putting in the tool allowance and the wet weather gear allowance," Hogan told *A Current Affair*, "because I was working on the Harbour Bridge … I had no money, and didn't care. I was happy, 'cause I never had to worry about keeping up with the Jones's … Overnight, I went right past the Jones's. They couldn't keep up with me!"

Ingeniously, Packer offered up a new Goliath for the Davids of western Sydney to rail against: the Australian Tax Office. This was ultimately the point of feasting on meat pies. Tax evasion replaced egalitarianism as the raison d'être of the Australian people. It became as manly as a cold beer and a punt at the pub. Australia's facade of classlessness stopped being a spontaneous compliment from silvertails to fibros and became part of a conscious PR strategy to promote the doctrine of inequality. Squatters realised that they could keep swagmen from fleecing their sheep by airbrushing the differences between them.

"Class in most places is about making the differences visible," says novelist Richard Flanagan, who grew up in a working-class mining community before receiving a Rhodes Scholarship to Oxford. "Class in Australia is about making the differences invisible."

That had been part of the point of larrikinism: to expose and attack those material differences, not minimise them. If the lucky country were truly egalitarian, the larrikin wouldn't have existed in the first place. Now, media tycoons and right-wing politicians recast a history of ratbags and rascals who wanted to overthrow the status quo into a fable about the mateship of Jack and his master. They were taking the piss out of egalitarianism. This new myth of the larrikin underpinned the Liberal Party's lie that Australia was a classless society.

Bob Hawke was the son of a congregational minister, not an Irish-Catholic convict. He had a relatively sheltered upbringing. His uncle Albert was the premier of Western Australia. His Bible-devouring mother believed Bob would lead Australia to greatness. "[Hawke] was like the Christ-child in Joseph's manger, whose mother had whispered in his ear at the age of five that he would be … the great prime minister and the great figure of Australia," Paul Keating told journalist Kerry O'Brien.

Hawke's brother Neil – the dux of King's College in Adelaide – died of meningitis at seventeen, heightening the smothering weight of expectation. At the same age that his older brother died, the now only child survived a near-fatal motorcycle accident. Bob Hawke joined the Australian Labor Party at the age of eighteen and took up drinking. He pursued influence, obliteration and physical intimacy with the urgency of someone who'd glimpsed the abyss.

Hawke did a bachelor of arts and a bachelor of laws at the University of Western Australia, was awarded a Rhodes Scholarship to Oxford and started a PhD at Australian National University. But the country he dreamed of leading suffered from chronic tall poppy syndrome. Nowhere chewed up and spat out lofty blossoms like Bob more voraciously than the labour movement. Men with soft hands and grandiose plans for world domination were seen at best as know-it-alls; at worst, flaming homosexuals. So Robert the Rhodes Scholar wore the mask of a working-class clown. "Hawkey" was born, an alter ego drawing upon all of Australia's deepest myths.

"The 'typical Australian' is a practical man," wrote Russel Ward in *The Australian Legend*, "rough and ready in his manners and quick to decry any appearance of affectation … He swears hard and consistently, gambles heavily and often, and drinks deeply on occasion … [He is] sceptical about the value of religion and of intellectual and cultural pursuits generally. He believes that Jack is not only as good as his master but, at least in principle, probably a good deal better, and so he is a great 'knocker' of eminent people unless, as in the case of his sporting heroes, they are distinguished by physical prowess."

Bob Hawke might have studied *The Australian Legend* like it was a cake recipe. He freely publicised his devotion to the four planks of Australian masculinity: sport, gambling, hitting the piss and promiscuity. He was a betting man with a missing gag reflex and a perpetual erection. By drinking all and sundry under the table, he liquidated the suspicions of blue-collar workers. This rendition of larrikinism was an act of conformism, not one of defiance.

"Bob was the world's number one drinker," former ACTU boss Bill Kelty told the ABC for the 2016 documentary *Bob Hawke: The Larrikin and the Leader*. "He could drink and drink and drink."

At Oxford, "Digger" finished 1.4 litres of beer in eleven seconds flat, a story so infamous that it seems trite to repeat it yet again. His capacity to drink like a fish kindled an unbreakable bond with the trade union movement and then the general public. He wasn't just someone punters wanted to have a beer with. He was someone punters imagined would want to have a beer with *them*. Luckily, most never actually got the chance. The consensus was that he acted like an absolute flog when on a bender.

"He was an alcoholic," Graham Richardson told *Bob Hawke: The Larrikin and the Leader*. "It was nothing for him to have twenty beers in a day. He did some appalling things when drunk … Some of the things were shocking. Just plain bloody shocking … Let's face it: a Bob Hawke today behaving in the same manner would never become prime minister."

Richardson isn't famous for populating the moral high ground. Richo was an Irish-Catholic true believer from the Sydney suburb of Kogarah, whose mother and father were trade union officials. Like Packer and Hawke, he survived a catastrophic accident as a teenager. At the age of eighteen, Packer was at the wheel of a car that collided head-on with another vehicle late at night, killing three people. Hawke, Richardson and Packer were a trio of Type A survivors. They had a similarly insatiable appetite for power. As warlord of the NSW Right, he cultivated mateships with media moguls such as Packer and John Singleton. KP and Singo belonged to a generation of entrepreneurial men – including Rupert Murdoch and Gerry Harvey – who pissed their money against the walls of open-secret gambling dens in Kings Cross. Hawkey was a fellow traveller.

"[Hawke] was a freak show," Singleton later told writer Derek Rielly. "Walked into a public bar at El Rancho at Epping one night when his driver was Graham Richardson, the later Minister for Health … We were having a few schooners after a TV show and the birds came from everywhere … I was just picking up the scraps."

Voters regarded Hawke's well-documented alcoholism and adultery as sources of authenticity, rather than proof of a lifelong identity crisis. There was actually something much more authentic about the unapologetically power-hungry Menzies, Whitlam and Fraser. That old-fashioned trio of pompous Presbyterians were scrupulously aloof from the attitudes of the battler.

Hawke consciously modelled himself as the antithesis of Menzies, Fraser and especially Whitlam, whom Labor desperately wanted the electorate to forget. While ACTU president, he secretly critiqued Whitlam's leadership to American diplomats, especially Gough's indifference to the existence of Israel. Hawke also leaked inside information about trade union strike plans that might affect American corporations, such as Ford. Solidarity forever!

"To [American diplomats], Hawke was an 'experienced chameleon' who had 'successfully played down his academic record and bookish background' and could transform into the 'ideal Australian Labor leader', despite his personal faults." So writes C.J. Coventry in a revealing recent article for the *Australian Journal of Politics and History*. This gap between perception and reality doesn't nullify Hawke's accomplishments. Progressive politics could do with a few more bullshit artists of his calibre. But nobody normal sincerely believes from a young age they will become the prime minister one day, let alone has the intellect or vanity to pull it off.

"His life took on such an overload, such a spin, such a public persona, which included a lot of socialising and a lot of drinking," ex-wife Hazel Hawke told the ABC documentary *Labor in Power*. "It was the distorted Bob that was a big problem. And unfortunately the children saw, I think, more of the distorted Bob than they saw of the real Bob that I knew was there. And that made me both very sad and very angry."

Fortunately for the Labor Party, Australians adored the distorted Bob Hawke. Australia's most decorated pisswreck became a teetotaller not for the sake of his wife and children, but for the grail of the prime ministership.

Hawke entered parliament in 1980 and unsuccessfully challenged Bill Hayden for the leadership of the Opposition in 1982. Hayden had spent two decades in parliament refining a social democratic policy platform. But his proletarian origins and policies didn't translate to TV. The Oxford-educated Hawke seemed far more ocker. "A lying cunt with a limited future," Hawke described Hayden in 1979, while Hawke was breaking up with Blanche d'Alpuget – one of several mistresses – because he didn't believe a divorced man could be prime minister.

"Divorce could cost Labor 3 per cent," he told d'Alpuget.

"I came to realise he was having affairs with women all over the country," she later wrote, "that his love life was a kind of free-wheeling, decentralised harem, with four or five favourites and a shoe-sale queue of one-night stands."

In March 1983, Malcolm Fraser attempted to outfox Hawke and his ruthless boosters by calling an early election. Disastrously for him, Hayden was literally in the middle of succumbing to the petitioning of colleagues, including mate John Button, a member of Victoria's Left faction. "In my experience in the Labor Party the fact that someone is a bastard … has never been a disqualification for the leadership," wrote Button.

By the time Fraser was granted an election by the governor-general, Hayden had bit the bullet and quit. "A drover's dog could lead the Labor Party to victory," he morosely quipped. A month before D-day, Labor was led not by a blind mutt, but by Australia's most charismatic bastard since Ned Kelly. The colony had long been run by a wowser majority. Hawke somehow turned his libidinousness into an electoral magic trick. Even Fraser's wife, Tamie, wasn't immune to temptation, calling her husband's enemy "sexy."

"Hawke used his sexuality as a seduction device on females or males, for personal as well as political purposes," says Phillip Adams. It is often said about larrikins that women want to be with them and men want to be like them. In the case of Hawke, it might be true to say that women wanted to root him and quite a few men wanted to root him too, betraying the deep homoerotic streak at the heart of Australian masculinity.

On 5 March 1983, the Labor Party won 49.48 per cent of the primary vote. Hawke took twenty-four seats from the Coalition. His stunning electoral success and unprecedented common touch turned federal politics into a pub test of presidential proportions, cursing leaders with the insane expectation that they needed to imitate the mannerisms of the degenerates who elect them.

Australia – a country supposedly cynical of authority and tall poppies – unconditionally forgave the new prime minister for his Machiavellian pursuit of power. Why? Bob Hawke was a larrikin. No, not just a larrikin; *The Larrikin*. His ocker accent emitted egalitarianism. His image radiated mateship. "Hawkey" was the grinning, swearing, sculling, rooting epitome of all the deepest myths we tell ourselves about what it takes to be a top bloke in the land down under.

Hawke cultivated the image of a sports-loving everyman. But his emotional attachment to Australia's football codes was overstated. Like Morrison, he was hamming it up for the cameras. "I had assumed from my first meeting with Hawke that he was a footy tragic," wrote George Megalogenis in *The Football Solution*. "But I realised later that his interest was not the football but the tipping … Football wasn't a passion of his … Which made him more like Paul Keating – a supporter of political convenience – than either man might concede."

In the wee hours of 27 September 1983, Bob Hawke sat at the Royal Perth Yacht Club, grinning like a Cheshire cat on pingers. He'd been prime minister since March. *Australia II* – the twelve-metre yacht owned by Alan Bond – had just won the America's Cup, the first time that another country's boat had done so. A reporter asked the prime minister if he'd had a cheeky flutter on the outcome. "The other day I just had a little bit on the trifecta for Hawthorn in Melbourne, Parramatta in Sydney and *Australia II*," he said, expertly appeasing football fans across both the southern and northern states. "Just a little bit."

At the age of eighteen, the British-born Alan Bond was caught burgling Perth homes while dressed as a meter reader. It was prophetic of the way swindlers like him would adopt blue-collar costumes to fleece ordinary people. He belonged to a generation of dodgy entrepreneurs who profited from Labor's deregulation of the financial sector. Bondy – a donor to the ALP – was a great mate of Hawkey and Richo. The blokeyness of phonies like Bond enabled Labor to masquerade crony capitalism as old-fashioned mateship.

At the yacht club, Hawkey – soon to receive a 75 per cent approval rating – united with a roomful of drunk yuppies for a passionate rendition of "Waltzing Matilda," a song about a suicidal homeless man who would rather drown in a swamp than brown-nose the authorities. Australia's most beloved recovering alcoholic was drenched with champagne on national TV.

"Bondy and all of ya there, we say well done, congratulations," said Hawkey. "I don't think there's been a greater moment of pride for Australia than what you've done. Not only winning, but the way you won ... It's one of the great moments in Australian history ... There are no group of Australians who deserve to be honoured more than this group."

According to Hawke, Bond's triumph eclipsed the miners' rebellion at Eureka, the striking shearers arriving in Longreach from Barcaldine, the suffragettes obtaining full enfranchisement for women first in the world, the diggers losing gallantly at Gallipoli before defeating the Japanese in New Guinea, Aboriginal and Torres Strait Islander Australians achieving full citizenship at the 1968 national referendum, or Gough Whitlam pouring red dirt through the fingers of Vincent Lingiari.

No: Australia's most unifying moment was a yacht belonging to Alan Bond passing the finish line first in the United States. It is difficult to imagine the people of Ipswich cheering much about the America's Cup. By 1980, the same year that caged canaries were made redundant by electric gas detectors, Ipswich was producing just 7 per cent of Queensland's coal, down from 80 per cent in 1902. In 1983, the Morris Woollen Mill was shut by tariff cuts, as cheaper and better-quality textiles from Asia flooded the domestic market. Trains were going electric, too, and it was cheaper to make the carriages and sleepers overseas. Bruce moved to Darwin to work at a power station. He went on strike within forty-eight hours of arrival. "Bond was a criminal," he says. "It's a disgrace Labor kissed the feet of pricks like him."

This was a victory for the New Believers: the capitalist and media class enamoured with a Labor Party still whipping itself silly for the sins of Gough Whitlam. Back at the Royal Perth Yacht Club, someone draped Hawke in a white blazer covered with national flags and the word *AUSTRALIA*.

"Any boss who sacks anyone for not turning up today is a bum!" he cackled, while in the midst of making it easier for such workers to get sacked. Hawke and Keating had embarked on dismantling Keynesianism as the underpinning principle of Australian politics, and not without some strong justifications. The Australian economy was well and truly rooted. So the dollar was floated. Tariffs got slashed and free trade agreements negotiated. Bankers and venture capitalists were given looser rein. Eventually, Qantas and the Commonwealth Bank were flogged off. The company tax rate was cut from 49 per cent to 36 per cent, and the top bracket of income tax cut from 60 per cent to 47 per cent.

"Labor stopped looking out for the interests of workers," says current president of the Australian Manufacturing Workers' Union Steve Murphy.

"It's pretty obvious that they bought into the neoliberal, free trade, privatisation, trickle-down economics fairytale."

The key difference between Thatcherism, Reaganism and Australia's brand of dinky-di deregulation was that Hawke could deliver the Prices and Incomes Accord, a ceasefire between the government and striking larrikins like Bruce. This meant he achieved reforms Reagan didn't dream of. In return, Labor promised workers stronger economic growth, and that it would provide a social wage: basically, tax cuts, Medicare and superannuation. But many skilled and unskilled labourers lost the incentive to be trade unionists, severing the umbilical cord between the working class and Labor.

John Black worked for the Australian Workers' Union. He prepared profiling for Hayden that helped win Hawke the 1983 election. In 1984, the Queenslander was elected to the Senate. He believes the Accord killed Labor's blue-collar base. "In the days when unions were all-pervasive, the members felt like they were a strong part of the Labor Party," Black tells me. "But blue-collar unions became weaker and weaker. They lost their power. They lost their mojo."

Bruce is still furious about the 1985 SEQEB dispute. Joh Bjelke-Petersen sacked 1001 employees of the South East Queensland Electrical Board, attempting to force permanent workers into contract labour. Ninety-six protestors were arrested. Bruce organised prawn and porn nights to raise funds. From Darwin, he donated 15 per cent of his wages to sacked comrades, along with Electrical Trades Union members around Australia. Bruce believes that Hawke reneged on a promise to defend his mates in the ETU.

"Hawke did sweet stuff-all," says Bruce. "That's when he lost me. Then he sacked all the Ansett pilots in '89. The unions were pretty much cactus. People like to blame Howard. But the rot started a long time before that."

The extinction of the radical larrikin correlated with the popularity of aesthetic larrikins like Hawkey, Bondy and Hoges. The PM intervened to approve his kindred spirit Hoges as the face of a Tourism Australia campaign. "Come and say g'day. I'll slip an extra shrimp on the barbie for ya."

During a 1980s boom in individualism, Australians grew nostalgic for Russel Ward's vanishing legend and projected a happy-go-lucky version of themselves to the world.

In 1985, Hoges imitated a digger in the TV series *Anzacs*. In 1986, *Crocodile Dundee* became America's second-highest grossing film of the year and the highest grossing Australian film of all time. The movie plagiarised the persona of a buffalo hunter named Rodney Ansell. In the late '70s, Ansell had survived seven weeks in the Northern Territory outback by sculling cattle blood. *The Guardian* later called him "a glorious anachronism who made a lone stand against soulless urbanization." He was a proto–One Nation voter.

Ansell begrudged Hollywood making hundreds of millions from identity theft while he kept going broke. When he advertised his farm as home to the real Crocodile Dundee, Hogan's representatives issued warnings. In 1999, Ansell went out in a blaze of mayhem. Camped beside a billabong, Ansell descended into speed addiction, a marriage between the unjolly swagman and Ned Kelly. He shot a copper before getting shot himself.

The fake Crocodile Dundee had long ago relocated to Los Angeles, where Hoges – glowing with botox and teeth whitener – embarked on a decade-long blood feud with the Australian Tax Office. Newspaper reports later claimed that he owed it $150 million in unpaid tax. The tall poppy hunter had been lopped down by gutless bureaucrats. He was mad as a cut snake.

"I want *not* to be picked on, *not* to be victimised because I'm high-profile and supposedly rich," said Hogan. "And therefore the tax office can demonstrate to Australia: *no one gets away with it. You cannot beat the tax man. These rich people and celebrities get special treatment.* I'm not Paris Hilton; I'm just Hoges! And all I've ever wanted was a fair go."

It was a moment of self-actualisation. The suicidal cop shooter had been usurped by the persecuted boomer as the truest expression of Australian values. Hogan's alter ego was a coping mechanism for globalisation. Mick Dundee bore no resemblance to the white-collar conmen fleecing retirees, the media tycoons lobbying for monopolies, or left-wing politicians accepting donations from their existential enemies. The lucky country clung to the outback larrikin hero, ashamed to admit we'd become a nation of fakes.

The same year that *Crocodile Dundee* smashed all the box office records, Hawke deregulated the media landscape. His great mate Kerry Packer was restricted to owning TV stations in Sydney and Melbourne. KP had been besmirched by Fairfax, which used the pseudonym "The Goanna" to accuse him of tax evasion and drug trafficking. Keating also had a bee in his bonnet about Fairfax. Hawke and Keating hatched an innovative way to attack a common enemy.

"Why don't you tell us precisely how you want to help your mates?" asked John Button in cabinet, with Bill Hayden the main objector.

"Remember they're the only mates we've got," said Bob Hawke.

Hawke and Keating created two monsters with a single piece of legislation: their changes allowed Packer to own TV stations in unlimited cities, and enabled Rupert Murdoch to purchase the Herald & Weekly Times, the largest newspaper company in the country. Murdoch — who had only recently renounced his Australian citizenship to live in America — controlled two-thirds of the Australian newspaper market. It was a shot across the bow of Fairfax by Labor. This was the definition of cutting off your nose to spite your face, or more accurately, of amputating your legs to fix itchy feet.

"As a consequence of the takeover, Australia now had a concentration of newspaper ownership unknown anywhere in the developed world beyond the party-controlled papers of the communist bloc," wrote Robert Manne in *The Monthly*. "In the short term, Labor was rewarded with the support of the three most popular Australian newspapers … In the long term it had been midwife at the birth of what was potentially the most anti-democratic force in national life and also the most powerful future enemy of Labor."

Packer reportedly sold the Nine Network to Alan Bond for $1 billion, shortly before the 1987 recession. It was a deal that cemented the immense wealth and the political power of the Packer empire. Three years later, Packer nabbed Channel Nine back for the $200 million that a bankrupted Bond owed him. The Big Man celebrated his enormous fortune by losing $20 million in a London gambling binge, and waging war on the ATO.

"I am not evading tax in any way, shape or form," he told bureaucrats at a corporate tax inquiry in 1991, while harbouring a fortune in offshore bank accounts. "Now, of course, I am minimising my tax and anybody in this country who doesn't minimise their tax, they want their heads read … I can tell you, you're not spending it that well that we should be donating extra."

Out of all the brash, fabricated larrikins evading tax and populating Australia's business and entertainment industries in the 1980s, Bond had the briefest longevity. He declared insolvency in 1992. In 1997, he was sentenced to seven years' prison for the theft of $1.2 billion. Hawke remained a life-long Bond apologist, and appeared at the thirtieth anniversary of the America's Cup victory in his famous white Australia jacket.

"You only get one Alan Bond," said Kerry Packer.

But Australia suffered from dozens of Alan Bonds, including Rene Rivkin, business partner of John Singleton and stockbroker for Kerry Packer. Richo rated Rivkin one of his five best mates, the ethical kiss of death. Rivkin was sitting at the VIP table with Hawke at Richo's retirement dinner in 1994.

"If you battle in Australia," said Richo, "you've only got one hope. And when there are millions of people battling, all of us must understand that the dignity of those battlers isn't worth something, it's worth everything."

Graham Richardson – called "The Minister for Channel Nine" while in cabinet – was quitting politics to work as a lobbyist for Packer. Hawke isn't responsible for the Swiss bank accounts of his numbers man, nor for the copycats Richo inspired within the NSW Right. But he must take some credit for leading Labor's embrace of flagrant fraudsters like Alan Bond. The toxic political culture that Hawke profited from became a template.

"I think [Hayden's removal] was a point at which the morality of the Labor Party was undermined," Neal Blewett, Hawke's minister for health, told the documentary *The Larrikin and the Leader*. "And I think that the philosophy which lay behind Hawke's decision – whatever it takes to win – triumphed … In a way, the Labor Party has suffered from that decay in its morality ever since."

More broadly, the Accord traded the socio-economic infrastructure provided by trade unions for the short-term approval of the capitalist class. In 1976, 51 per cent of the workforce belonged to a union. The figure was down to 31 per cent by 1996 and 14 per cent by 2016. The Accords put the cart of the Labor Party before the horse of the labour movement.

"Labor started losing working-class voters during the Hawke years," says John Black. "Blue-collar workers didn't like the outcomes. The middle class did … Labor won more votes in middle-class urban seats."

The biggest beneficiaries of deregulation were Labor's existential enemies, including News Limited, the gravest danger of all. Unfortunately, you can only sell your soul to the devil once. Without millions of fibros willing to strike for higher pay, Labor had nothing left to trade with the silvertails or media tycoons.

There were millions of working-class winners too. In Ipswich, my parents met in 1979. Dad was about to declare bankruptcy after a disastrous first marriage. Mum – the daughter of a war veteran on a pension – worked with Bruce's mum Ivy at Woolworths. She fell pregnant. Dad applied for a divorce under Whitlam's changes to the *Marriage Act*. Nearing retirement, coalminer John lent my father $7000 of life savings to buy a taxi licence.

My father was an aspirational. He was pathologically obsessed with escaping the proletariat and leaving behind a financial legacy. Dad hated university-educated silvertails. But he wanted his children to be silvertails so badly that he was prepared to work eighty-hour weeks – and ultimately into an early grave – to make it happen. In Hawke and Keating's Australia, small business owners such as him didn't need to rely on loans from old coalminer mates. Foreign money flooded the financial sector and made it easier for aspirationals to buy businesses and investment properties.

"Without Keating's reforms, we'd be a much poorer and more white-bread-eating, missionary-rooting outpost of England," says Lachlan Harris, a former press secretary to Kevin Rudd, and founder of the Budgy Smuggler brand. "And we'd look like a blander, shitter version of the larrikin that the major parties paint us to be, rather than the quite interesting, innovative, diverse country that we actually are."

Mum and Dad gradually escaped the working class of their upbringings. Economic rationalism divided Labor's blue-collar base into two camps: the millions of cashed-up bogans like my parents who benefited from the new money, and the millions of ropable bogans who lost their permanent jobs and stable sense of identity. Labor lost a bunch of the winners to the Liberal Party. Meanwhile, the losers sharpened a hatchet for Paul Keating, Australia's brashest aspirational.

Bob Hawke robbed Ipswich of its potential prime minister, and its voters later repaid Labor by electing Pauline Hanson to the seat of Oxley. But first, Bill Hayden had cursed his assassin with a more immediate threat: a feverishly ambitious shadow treasurer, who promised "massive retaliation" if Hawke demoted him from the shadow treasurership.

Paul Keating grew up in Bankstown, which he described as "the land of the fibro house." "You can be on the side of the angels – that's the great body of working people – or you can be on the side of … the people with capital and position," Keating told Kerry O'Brien in 2016. "I wanted to lift 95 per cent of the people up, not 5 per cent. I didn't want to lift up Bellevue Hill and Vaucluse."

Keating was a street-smart hustler from the western suburbs. His lust for power was accompanied by a bulletproof armour of self-regard and moral righteousness. Keating's mother and grandmother smothered him with love. He compared their industrial-strength affection to wearing an asbestos suit into a fire. His father, Matt, was an aspirational battler, who escaped the safe bet of the railway for the risk and reward of private enterprise. By the late 1950s, the business Matt Keating started employed fifty people. Paul – his only son – left high school at the age of fourteen, eschewing formal study.

"Bob used to often say to me: oh, you should get out and meet the public," Keating told O'Brien in 2014. "Bob went from university to Oxford and shoehorned into the ACTU … I worked in the Sydney County Council in Sydney for the first six years of my working life amongst fitters and turners and labourers. The life was so raw and ribald you couldn't put it across on national television. Believe me, you wouldn't get any of that in a university."

The Rhodes Scholar spoke like a fibro from the western suburbs. The Bankstown battler had the cultural inclinations of an Oxford-educated aristocrat. They had asymmetrical insecurities. Hawke was desperate to be regarded as the most macho man in the country, and Keating as the smartest.

"[Keating] had no passion for sport," wrote historian Don Watson in *Recollections of a Bleeding Heart*. "More than that, he thought its pre-eminence in Australian culture was a threat to the nation's collective intelligence."

Hawke adopted the posture of a larrikin, but deep down he was a people-pleaser. For Keating, anti-authoritarianism was a spiritual compulsion. The odd couple was greater than the sum of their parts. Labor needed a fanatical treasurer to navigate the parliament and public service, and a loveable larrikin to maintain party morale and public support. They bridged their innate differences for the better part of eight years, although privately the relationship frayed. By 1988, Keating sought the Kirribilli Agreement: a formal assurance that Hawke would stand aside after the 1990 election.

Bob Hawke survived the near-miss 1990 election thanks to an unlikely alliance between Labor's Graham Richardson and the Greens' Bob Brown. Australia slumped into recession. Treasurer Keating plunged into a black fog of fury about the prime minister's lack of urgency to honour the Kirribilli Agreement. In December, Keating delivered his infamous Plácido Domingo speech to the press gallery. He claimed Australia had never been led by a truly great leader. "Leadership is not about being popular," said Keating. "It's about being right … And it's not whether you go through some shopping centre tripping over the TV crew's cords."

In hindsight, Keating calling John Curtin a "trier" was probably less unpatriotic than Hawke bitching about Whitlam to American diplomats while Gough was still the prime minister, or Hawke nominating winning the America's Cup as the single greatest moment in Australian history. But emotions were running high, and Hawke jubilantly reneged on the Kirribilli Agreement. According to the PM, Keating called Australia "the arsehole of the world" while pleading for him to quit. Their battle devolved into a dispute about who loved Australia more. "[Hawke] always thought that he knew the Australian people better than anyone else," said Keating in *Labor in Power*. "I'll back my loyalty to this country and my patriotism against Bob Hawke's any day."

By Christmas 1991, Paul Keating was prime minister. Bob Hawke moved into John Singleton's mansion. The right-wing silvertail – who oversaw Labor's advertising campaigns in 1987 and 1990 – taught the humbled everyman how to purchase a carton of milk.

Hawke's monogamous replacement was begrudgingly respected by the electorate, but far from beloved. The Tories gave Keating twin gifts: an Opposition leader more aesthetically out of touch than him, and an economic agenda – titled Fightback! – even less sympathetic to the losers from economic deregulation than Labor's. "This is the sort of little-boy, stamp your foot stuff which comes from a financial yuppie when you shoo him into parliament," said Keating.

The Opposition leader, John Hewson, had attended Kogarah State High. His father was a fitter and turner. The viciousness of the prime minister's attacks on a fellow aspirational battler were by Keating's own admission pragmatic, but perhaps partly driven by a fibro's self-loathing for how far he'd flown from the Bankstown days. "At the time we were living in Double Bay and Keating was living in Elizabeth Bay," Hewson later protested to Fairfax. "I could almost throw a stone from my house to his. He had a Mercedes and, OK, I had a Ferrari."

Translation: we are all aspirationals now.

Artificial class war papered over Labor's existential crisis. Keating's economic agenda was loathed by fibros and beloved by silvertails. But Hewson cocked up the unloseable election with a GST. Keating was determined to splurge his political capital on worthy fights. He endorsed the ethically correct but socially divisive causes of reconciliation, multiculturalism and the republic. He called out the Anzac Myth as an empire-building exercise. He slaughtered sacred cows of white Australia with sneering disregard for the hurt feelings of Protestant snobs. Bronwyn Bishop – a fifth-rate silvertail from the North Shore – compared this brilliant yet malicious shit-stirrer to Ned Kelly. Keating's speechwriter Don Watson discreetly agreed.

"In his occasional self-destructive rages, his intemperate speech, his radical vision, his Irish loathing of the Establishment and his odd old-world honour, Paul Keating was like Ned Kelly," wrote Watson. "Like Ned he had the Irishman's 'fanatic heart.'"

Tragically, fibros with Such Is Life tattoos saw Paul Keating as the tallest poppy of all. He attracted a poisonous following of socialist silvertails with booming superannuation portfolios. Gough's Aristocrats gave birth to Keating's Elites. White-collared and privately insured, Keating's Elites had little interest in the humdrum subjects of industrial relations or public hospitals. They could afford wholehearted support for environmental causes, as none of their jobs were under threat. Many saw voting for Labor not as a survival mechanism, but as a personality type, a more socially enlightened version of Menzies' moral middle class.

"Fibros in western Sydney saw Labor pandering to rugby union fans," says Roy Masters, who admired Keating, but not the passengers he attracted. "Labor started listening too much to silvertails who went to the best private schools. They live on the North Shore. They drink chardonnay, not beer. They focus on issues that give them some degree of moral superiority. But I doubt if they'd share a dollar from their wallet. And they despise rugby league fans."

Rugby league was the only expression of working-class pride millions of fibros in the northern states had left. Most of Labor's True Believers had stopped believing in God. Trade unions cut a deal with bosses to suppress wage growth. The Labor Party adopted a neoliberal policy agenda that sacrificed unskilled manufacturing jobs for free trade agreements.

Steve Murphy, the president of the AMWU, is from Irish-Catholic stock and was born and raised in the Hunter Valley. His father switched from building trains for the South Maitland Railway to a job at Bradmill, where he met Murphy's mother. Bradmill, a textile factory, was hammered by redundancies in the 1990s, and later bought by National Textiles. John Howard's brother Stan was chairman of National Textiles when the factory went bust in 2000. Steve Murphy says Stan ran it into the ground, but he also blames tariff cuts by the Hawke–Keating government.

"They used to say that Labor was freeing workers from the production line," says Murphy. "Well, they freed us from the production line to go into low-paid, insecure, subservient work. And for what? So that we could buy a washing machine for seventy bucks cheaper? It's not a fair trade."

Rupert Murdoch was determined to make rugby league a profit enhancer for private capital. In 1993, Kerry Packer got the pay-TV rights to the NSW Rugby League for peanuts from its CEO, John Quayle, the man who took Packer to his first footy game. Murdoch tried to obtain those rights for his fledgeling Foxtel. Packer threatened to sue the pants off Murdoch, and the NSWRL if it entertained his approach. So Murdoch secretly recruited eight teams from the Australian Rugby League to start a rival competition called Super League. Part-time players with blue-collar jobs were offered six-figure contracts.

At the time, Steve Murphy was doing an apprenticeship as a fitter machinist at South Maitland Railways. Two of his workmates – Darren Albert and Mark Hughes – secured inflated deals from the Packer-aligned ARL. "Rupert Murdoch tried to tear apart working-class culture," he says. "Once Super League happened, rugby league was all for profit."

The highest-paid player for Murdoch's Super League was Allan Langer, my first cousin. "Alfie" was Queensland's most beloved larrikin. He dropped out of school at the end of Grade Ten. The railway no longer provided a limitless supply of apprenticeships. My mother got him a job as a furniture removalist. He might've ended up on the bones of his arse in the impending recession. But the shy fibro won the lottery: a champion athlete, he became Australia's first million-dollar-a-year footballer, and a prominent pawn in Murdoch's propaganda war with Packer.

Packer's highest-paid pawn was a fibro from Penrith named Bradley Fittler, the son of a single mum. Fibro "Freddy" went from earning $160,000 a year, to a five-year, $600,000-per-annum contract with a $300,000 bonus. He bought a block on the Northern Beaches and signed to play in the eastern suburbs. "I no longer saw the northern beaches or the eastern suburbs as a foreign land," said an honest Fittler. "In fact, I couldn't think of anything better than moving out of [Penrith] and settling in a house on the beach."

This was to be the paradox of aspirational Australia: fibros from Ipswich and Penrith were dying to be silvertails, while Bellevue Hill billionaires like Packer profited from masquerading as Australian legends. The trick was to let enough battlers slip through the net that all of them would believe they could be millionaires – but not enough to narrow the growing gap between rich and poor.

The Super League war was a false war, to borrow a phrase from Menzies. Kerry was just trying to drive Rupert's price up. James Packer and Lachlan Murdoch maintained amicable contact throughout the bitter PR and legal battle. Eventually, James and Lachlan organised for their fathers to meet on a yacht in the Bay of Plenty. Packer's mask slipped, and he cut a deal. Rugby league was forced into a shotgun marriage with News Corp. Six Sydney teams were merged into three. The South Sydney Rabbitohs – the team Packer fell in love with while eating a pie at Redfern Oval – was kicked out of the competition.

NSW premier Bob Carr – notoriously agnostic towards sport – said it had nothing to do with politics. Only two Labor MPs spoke out against News Corp's annexation of working-class culture: Mark Latham and Anthony Albanese. In 1971, an eight-year-old Albanese had watched the South Sydney Rabbitohs win the league grand final at the SCG with his single mum. He joined the board of the Rabbitohs after they were kicked out, and attacked News Corp in parliament.

"The decision by the National Rugby League to exclude South Sydney from the 2000 competition leaves the faceless men who run the game with red-and-green blood on their hands," he said in the House of Representatives. "It is about whether the dollar can override all human and social relationships."

The dispute sparked a march by 80,000 rugby league fans in Sydney. After losing in the courts, and facing a backlash from its NSW readership, News Corp surrendered. The Rabbitohs returned to the NRL in 2002 and won the grand final in 2014. Souths made Albo a life member. He belonged to a small group of diehards who saved the club from extinction.

"Making an enemy out of an organisation like News Limited – it's okay to do that when you're a lawyer or a media star," Nick Pappas – the son of Greek refugees and current chairman of the Rabbitohs – told journalist Karen Middleton. "But when you're a politician and your fate sort of rests securely on how you're presented in the media on a day-to-day basis, that requires a lot of fortitude."

The Super League war was a horrifying metaphor for the forthcoming Culture War supervised by Uncle Rupert. News Corp threw crumbs to a few winners and started a quagmire of fights between rival tribes of fibros, who forgot they could get a much larger slice of the overall pie by sticking together. While a working-class institution burned, a couple of Geelong Grammar old boys retired to a yacht and carved up the winnings.

The reign of John Howard was made and maintained by two leaders: Paul Keating and Pauline Hanson. Pauline got her surname from Mark Hanson, a plumber from Ipswich, and an old rugby league chum of my father's. Following their separation, she was a struggling single mum running a flourishing Ipswich fish-and-chip shop. "Then the Vietnamese started to move into the fish-and-chip-shop business," Hanson later bemoaned to documentary-maker Anna Broinowski. "A lot of them didn't speak the English language at all, and they were very much to themselves."

Ipswich – heavily unionised and tremendously Anglo – had been a key target audience for the White Australia policy. At the same time Asian faces appeared on Queensland streets, manufacturing jobs were smashed by the slashing of tariffs. It wasn't *purely* that the newcomers had a different skin colour, although there was a high baseline level of xenophobia. It was also the instinct that an army of migrants – whose kids seemed smarter and better mannered – were jumping the queue for the vanishing supply of reliable jobs. The triumphalism of white pride was a smokescreen for a crippling sense of inferiority.

There was a fresh batch of redundancies on the Ipswich railway. The local unemployment rate hit 11 per cent. The existential simplicity of working with your mates in the same factory or coalmine as your parents was replaced by the highly paid social isolation of FIFO, a casual job in the services industry, or the dole. The net result was an atomised proletariat, denied not just the fruits of their labour but the social ties that had alleviated alienation and enabled collective action.

In 2017, for *Meanjin*, writer Shannon Burns diagnosed the psychological appeal of right-wing populism to the "bad, white working class" he belonged to as a kid on the economically depressed outskirts of Adelaide. Burns wrote: "If a well-dressed, university-educated middle-class person … so much as hinted at my 'white privilege' while I was a lumpen child, or my 'male privilege' while I was an unskilled labourer who couldn't afford basic necessities, or my 'hetero-privilege' while I was a homeless solitary, I'd have taken a special pleasure in voting for their nightmare."

In 1994, Hanson was elected to Ipswich Council as the anti-library candidate. A year later, Labor staged a coup against her, and she left again. But she loved the conflict of politics. It was at this point that Hanson inadvertently emerged into the ideological vacuum created by the local lumpenproletariat's loathing of the clock connoisseur from Bankstown. "I thought [Keating] was an arrogant man," Hanson later told Broinowski. "He didn't understand how the Australian people were feeling."

To gain preselection for the Liberal Party in the seat of Oxley, Hanson needed to knock off my uncle George. George was a cashed-up bogan. He left school at twelve for an apprenticeship as a painter on the Ipswich railway. He left the railway to start a house-painting business with my father, a partnership that ended with fisticuffs. Dad cashed out way too prematurely. George became stinking rich and switched political camps, the black sheep of a left-wing family. In 1993, this tattooed Tory ran for the Liberal Party in the Ipswich electorate of Oxley.

"I started off in the railway as an apprentice and then I went out on my own,'" Uncle George, a real-life Ayn Rand character, once told *The Queensland Times*. "During Expo [Expo '88] I had sixty-five men employed. I put thirty-two apprentices through their apprenticeships and with no government assistance, I did it all myself."

My father – later a Labor branch president in Toowoomba – was stoked when his turncoat older brother failed to win Bill Hayden's old seat in 1993. He was doubly delighted when the Tories sacked George for Pauline. She had Buckley's of winning the ALP's safest seat in Queensland. Labor missed the disillusionment of True Believers, and so did the Coalition. They replaced a neoliberal technocrat from Rose Bay with a Tory aristocrat from Adelaide. Alexander Downer became their shortest-serving leader. The last man left standing was John Howard, a veteran loser who became skipper for the second time in January 1995. He was the only modern politician more fawning about the virtues of ordinary people than Bob Hawke.

"Howard would go to a leagues club for a dinner of rubber chicken, and he wasn't trying to be interested in the people there," says Geoff Cousins, a maverick advertising guru who became a personal adviser to Howard. "He genuinely liked them. Even Hawkey didn't approach Australians in quite the same way. He still had a sense of intellectual superiority. Howard didn't."

Little Johnny was drier than a dog shit left in the sun too long. He displayed none of Keating's wit or Hawke's virility, nor any of the born-to-rule gravitas of Fraser, Whitlam and Menzies. Which was precisely what many bogans in suburban and regional Australia liked about the bloke. Many of them had traded jobs on a factory floor for casual and often solitary employment. DUI laws ruled out sinking a skinful at the pub, so they savoured a six-pack while watching *Friday Night Football* alone. They harboured dreams of home ownership and the occasional budget holiday to the coast. They didn't want to be inspired, impressed or lectured. They wanted to be listened to and respected. Most of all, those lonely fibros wanted to belong to a team again.

"Where Keating spoke *to* the nation," wrote Liberal historian Judith Brett in *Relaxed and Comfortable*, "Howard spoke from it – straight from the heart of its shared beliefs and commonsense understandings of itself. This is revealed in the images which surround the two men. Keating's are of foreignness – his Italian suits, his love of German music and French clocks. Howard's are of suburban ordinariness – barbeques, cricket, the annual holiday at the same beachside resort, jogging in a shiny tracksuit festooned with logos."

Howard was a silvertail in fibro clothing. He received a ringing endorsement from Packer, that peerless chameleon. "I think he's an honest man," said Packer on *A Current Affair*. "I think he's a decent man." KP taught Honest John that the easiest way to assimilate with the working class was to wear tracksuits and gaze passionately at athletes. Alan Jones was Packer's highest-paid employee. He lived in a penthouse opposite the Opera House nicknamed "The Toaster." Howard was his favorite reactionary since Joh Bjelke-Petersen. From Jones, Howard gleaned that the single-minded pursuit of power could be camouflaged by adopting the monotonous rhetoric of the underdog. Now, Howard somehow turned a vote for the Liberal

Party into a *fuck you* to Bellevue Hill and Toorak, while keeping those core constituencies onside with the fait accompli of tax cuts.

Howard's Forgotten People were beer-drinking, sports-loving patriots. He offered them unconditional mateship. Howard's Battlers were tired of change and sick of being dobbed on and snickered at by snobs who got all of the pay rises and overseas holidays from globalisation, but none of the job insecurity. Their supreme leader glorified aspects of their existence that others saw as fatal flaws, and forgave them unconditionally for racism, both casual and systematic. "Don't any of you ever be lectured by the Labor Party about racial tolerance, never, ever," said Howard during the 1996 election campaign.

Hanson's electoral prospects skyrocketed the moment she was disendorsed by the Liberals for attacking Aboriginal people. Oxley's unemployment rate remained at 10.7 per cent, and a vast majority of the jobless were white settlers, not Jagera, Yuggera or Ugarapul people. Hanson's obsession with minority entitlements struck a chord precisely because so many of her white acolytes – or their family members – needed welfare during the process of deindustrialisation, and the following bust. They weren't debt-and-deficit fetishists, but self-loathing dole bludgers comforting themselves that the minorities who needed government support were lazy, unlike them and their kin: hard workers ripped off by greedy politicians.

Rachel Nolan is a former Labor state MP for the seat of Ipswich, and now a director of the McKell Institute, a social democratic think-tank. "Labor people rightly lionise Paul Keating as the architect of modern Australia," she says, "but we shouldn't get misty-eyed about the reality of the transition for working-class communities. Ipswich people hated economic deregulation and they were never convinced Keating's social agenda would lead to meaningful employment for them or their families.

In a battle between a Zegna-wearing Ned Kelly and Robert Menzies in tracksuit pants, a nation of self-proclaimed larrikins voted overwhelmingly for a paternalistic nerd who offered them the democratic version of a Valium. Howard turned black sheep like Uncle George into a herd. A generation of men who looked and sounded "working class" had ditched unionised jobs for small businesses. Tradies voted with their hip pockets. The tranquilised larrikins emerged as the hi-vis kingmakers of Australian politics, because they became willing to swing at the drop of a hat.

Howard – the opposite of a tall poppy – won twenty-nine seats from Labor. Twenty-one of them were located in New South Wales and Queensland. Ten of those electorates were either regional or rural. By contrast, the Liberal landslide picked up only two seats apiece in Victoria, South Australia and Western Australia. The centre of gravity in Australian politics had shifted decisively from the south to the north, from the cities to the suburbs and regions, from the bureaucrats to the blue-collar battlers, and from fashionable politicians to ones who could simulate an affinity with the masses. It seems highly unlikely the Liberal Party would have won so handsomely in Queensland with a Victorian leader such as Howard enemies Andrew Peacock or Jeff Kennett, two elite private schoolboys who radiated self-admiration, much like Menzies and Fraser before them.

"I don't think Peter Costello would have swept the rugby league states in quite the same way," said John Fahey, who won the western Sydney seat of Macarthur for the Liberals with an 11.97 per cent swing. "Victorians always thought they were better than New South Welshmen. New South Wales Libs were a bit more down-to-earth. John Howard liked Queenslanders, and they liked him."

By grudgingly sacking Hanson a week before the big dance, Howard gave vindictive Labor voters in Oxley a hall pass to lodge a protest vote against economic rationalism. Those ideological renegades united with the seat's minority of dyed-in-the-wool conservatives to elect Hanson with 54.66 per cent of the two-party-preferred vote. Post-Keating, Oxley returned safely to Labor.

"Pauline Hanson retold snatches of [Banjo Paterson and Henry Lawson] with gusto late last century, and many Australians still hankered for them," wrote Melissa Lucashenko. "So long as the illusion of the Good Old Days held, so did One Nation, to an extent, but alas for Pauline that story was all too quickly replaced by an even older tale, that of the Hand in the Till."

In 2003, Hanson spent eleven weeks in prison for electoral fraud. But One Nation was a cockroach that couldn't be crushed. In 1996, the result was easily dismissed as random Queenslanders being routine rednecks. From 2021, the fall of Oxley looks more like a prophecy. Hanson's rise awakened a cross-continental tide of nationalism that the Liberals would ride to government in nineteen of the next twenty-five years. "It has been widely recognised by all, including the media, that John Howard sailed home on One Nation policies," she told *The Age*.

The lessons of her election aren't merely domestic. Two decades before Brexit and Trump, Ipswich blew a premature smoke signal of the fury brewing towards Third Way parties from blue-collar communities whose stable sense of economic security and cultural hegemony was systematically eviscerated by free trade and high immigration rates.

"Ipswich is a magnificently prescient exemplar of everything going wrong everywhere else in the English-speaking world," says Rachel Nolan.

The blasé patriotism of Hawke was a gateway drug to Howard's avid nationalism. Race explains much about Howard's enduring popularity, but not everything. Allegedly redneck electorates in Queensland stuck with Labor after Whitlam embraced Lingiari and Keating made the Redfern Speech, while the small-l liberals of Sydney and Melbourne kept voting for reactionaries. But by 1996, too many battlers couldn't distinguish between the parties on the economy. So they voted for the leader who offered them the keenest sense of belonging. For swung voters, culture trumped class only once they didn't trust the Labor Party to defend their jobs for dear life.

"In 1998, there's a state election at which One Nation win eleven seats, but Labor regains government," says Nolan. "That happened because Peter Beattie rejected One Nation's racism, while promising to cut unemployment from 10 per cent to 5 per cent. Politics is all about low-skilled and semi-skilled jobs."

Menzies awakened the middle class. Howard converted the working class. And thanks to Keating, who modernised the economy to the nth degree, Howard had barely any blood on his hands for economic rationalism. He did much more than hold the fort. The Coalition flogged off

Telstra and introduced a GST, charging fibros for buying meat pies so that silvertails could get more company and personal tax cuts. The Liberal base also received a raft of new loopholes to minimise the capital gains within their property, stock and superannuation portfolios. Howard squandered the longest boom in Australian history on middle-class welfare and fresh incentives for aspirational families to embrace private education and health. And he relentlessly attacked the enfeebled trade unions.

"The Liberals claim they're the party of the battler," says Steve Murphy, who had left his trade to work for the AMWU by the early 2000s. "They fucking created us! We faced three waves of industrial relations legislation designed to make sure that working-class people lost all of their workplace power and the ability to improve their quality of life … Is that a 'fair go'?"

The Coalition crafted an election-winning combination of small-l liberal tall poppies in the cities, cashed-up tradies in the suburbs and hi-vis miners in regional Western Australia and Queensland. According to John Black, miners started departing the Labor Party in 1966 and were a net negative for the ALP by 1998. Bruce spent the boom working FIFO as a sparkie on mines near Chinchilla and Gladstone.

"It all changed," he says. "The miners in Ipswich joined a union and voted Labor. But young ones coming through didn't think of themselves as working class. They moved to the Sunny Coast. Four-bedroom house. Couple of cars. Most of them became anti-union! Dumb fucks thought they got paid 200 k just because they're good at their jobs. Nothin' to do with my generation and me dad's generation, and the sacrifices we made by going on strike."

The ALP couldn't win. The unskilled workers who lost their reliable jobs due to tariff cuts and privatisation blamed Labor for forsaking them. They became the target for One Nation. By sandbagging potential One Nation voters, Labor lost a generation of inner-city progressives to the Greens. Meanwhile, the skilled tradies who became millionaires from Keating's economy switched to the Liberals, because their tax bill would always be lower under the old enemy.

"This has happened since Karl Marx was a boy," says John Black.

Howard got all of the glory from the higher growth and rising dollar. Everyone was a winner, almost, and the Coalition knew how to recruit the losers too. The Liberals increased skilled migration to record levels, while the Nationals attracted sacked factory workers and underpaid farmhands in country towns, who blamed welfare recipients, refugees and Islamic jihadists for their diminishing standards of living.

"Conservatives played tricks on working-class people to divide us every day of the week," says Murphy. "They stoked this fear of the unknown. And they were gonna save us from it. The attacks on bludgers, the attacks on Muslims, the children overboard, the race riots."

Abdul Abdullah was born in 1986. Abdullah was the youngest sibling of four: an older sister named Rabiah and two older brothers named Abdul. For stealing two stamps and a watch chain, great-great-great-great-grandfather Charles Blinman – on their father's side – was sent to Australia on *The Indefatigable*. He lived at the Hero of Waterloo Hotel in The Rocks. Five generations later, Abdul's white dad met and fell in love with a Muslim woman named Maimunah in Malaysia. She moved back to Perth. Her husband converted to Islam and changed his name to Ibrahim. They raised a family in East Cannington, a working-class suburb of Perth.

"We were the three Bs: broke, brown and beautiful," says Abdullah, who has a mullet, moustache and the high-pitched cackle of a larrikin. "I was always a bit of a misfit. It was a rough neighbourhood. There were Aboriginals, Muslims, Asians, Islanders and Aussies. Muslims were a bit eccentric, because our dads had long beards. But everyone was dirt-poor, so nobody gave much of a fuck. Then 9/11 happened. And we became an existential threat."

After watching the towers come down, Abdullah and his brothers kept playing Gran Turismo, believing the hijacked planes had little to do with them. The next day, on 12 September, their mother Maimunah caught the train to volunteer with refugees. She was chased into a shop by a mob of white men, who spat racial obscenities and ripped her headscarf off. The anger from Perth patriots was indiscriminate: they also threw a pig's head at a local Sikh temple. "Dickheads," Abdullah says.

He was fifteen when the towers went down. His mum stopped wearing her face scarf in public. Their youngest son was singled out more by teachers, security guards and coppers for running amok. White kids were larrikins. Muslim kids were criminals. Their demonisation allowed the Liberal Party to invade two countries and get re-elected.

"When you're from a community like mine," says Omar Sakr, "you always have the awareness that the country you are a citizen of is actively engaged in murdering people like you in other countries. And using all the narratives around terrorists – and the supposed values of the Arab-Muslim community – to justify the increasingly cruel treatment of refugees here."

Omar Sakr grew up in Liverpool, southwestern Sydney, the son of Turkish and Lebanese migrants. He was raised in council housing: first by an auntie, then by his mother – both single mums. Sakr struggled with childhood trauma and undiagnosed ADHD. He didn't have enough money to maintain mental and dental health. His happiest memories from a poverty-stricken childhood were attending Canterbury Bulldogs games at Belmore Oval. "We were visibly fucking ecstatic, playing the drums and quite literally dancing," says Sakr. "In a time when we had all this hate being directed at us as a community, it's one of the main sources of joy I can recall."

One of Sakr's sole pleasures was destroyed by public demonisation of Canterbury Bulldogs fans – generally identified as "Lebs" – for their anti-social behaviour. The police presence at Bulldogs games grew too overbearing for many Lebanese-Australian fans. "Lebs are just Arabic bogans," says Sakr. "From the trackies to the singlets and mullets. They couldn't be more Australian if they fucking tried."

The rising nationalism of John Howard's aspirational Australia reached a surreal apotheosis in December 2005. Alan Jones had left Packer's 2UE for Singleton's 2GB. That summer, Jones whipped white larrikins from the southern suburbs into a fury about brown larrikins from the western suburbs flooding the beaches of Cronulla. The warring factions didn't see their similarities. The shock jocks and News Corp journalists promoted racial solidarity over class solidarity.

"All rhetoric, no action," said Alan Jones on 7 December, quoting a concerned citizen named John. "My suggestion is to invite one of the biker gangs to be present in numbers at Cronulla Railway Station when these Lebanese thugs arrive. It'd be worth the price of admission to watch these cowards scurry back onto the train for the return trip to their lairs … Australians old and new shouldn't have to put up with this scum."

Four days later, 5000 larrikins — generally white men under the age of twenty-five — descended on Cronulla, envisioning themselves as latter-day re-enactors of the Gallipoli landing, except their enemies were unarmed. The angry mob chanted "Fuck off, Lebs" and "Aussie Aussie Aussie Oi Oi Oi" between renditions of "Advance Australia Fair" and "Waltzing Matilda." They ripped the headscarf from a young woman on the sand dunes and hunted down two men of Middle Eastern appearance to the train station, where the enemy were punched, kicked and bottled.

"It was a patriarchal pissing contest between white men who were very upset that brown men were getting with 'their' girls," says Sakr.

The violence threatened to brew into a turf war between Lebs from western Sydney and the Bra Boys, a heavily tattooed surf gang from the beachside suburb of Maroubra. A peace deal was brokered by two senior members who'd spent time in Long Bay prison together. They had an epiphany: their common enemy was the coppers. "We've never ever backed these things against the Lebanese community," said a Bra Boy at a public appearance with Arabic members of the Comanchero Motorcycle Club. "Never! We never have, and we never will … We don't protect police. Full stop." Solidarity forever!

Abdul Abdullah channelled rage from a racially charged coming-of-age into art classes and boxing training. His sister ran a boxing gym. His brother-in-law was a state boxing champion and silver medalist for Australia at the Oceania Games. At the height of the mining boom, Abdullah went to fight nights. "You'd see tables of bikies all dressed like real estate agents," he tells me, "and tables of real estate agents carrying on like bikies. The bikies had been through metal detectors. They were on their best behaviour. Whereas the real estate agents would be swaggering around like real tough guys."

Abdullah describes himself as an outsider among outsiders. He was too art-school at the boxing gym and too working-class at art school. He belonged to a country that valorised the convicts and diggers on his dad's side. But that larrikin tradition denied him membership due to his mum's race and religion, while embracing billionaires like Kerry Packer.

"'Waltzing Matilda' showed the Australian class system," he says. "You've got the swagman from the convict class. Then you've got the coppers. The coppers are working at the behest of the squatters, who own the land. But now you've got all these people with power pretending to be larrikins."

Two weeks after the Cronulla Riots, Kerry Packer went cold turkey on treatment for kidney disease. "This is my time," he told Alan Jones, his deathbed confidante. The billionaire was right: the next day, Packer blinked away into extinction, eliciting inadmissible sighs of relief from the employees and politicians he had terrorised with an iron fist, and from family members who lied through their teeth after he died about his heart of gold.

The prime minister offered to throw the atheist billionaire a $70,000 state memorial service, an honour usually reserved for public officials. And where better to hold it than the Sydney Opera House, an upper-class echo chamber built from the proceeds of a lottery? White sails, blue body of water. God is dead and greed's an absolute goer.

Jonesy was the master of ceremonies. James Packer, John Howard and Russell Crowe did eulogies. Tom Cruise and Katie Holmes showed their support for a grief-stricken heir. James Packer suffocated under a weight of expectation. Malcolm Turnbull came to bury the hatchet.

"He did threaten to kill me," Turnbull confessed to Annabel Crabb in her 2009 Quarterly Essay, regarding Packer's attempted takeover of Fairfax, which was thwarted by subterfuge from Turnbull. "And I said to him, 'Well. You better make sure that your assassin gets me first because if he misses, you better know I won't miss you.' He could be a complete pig, you know … But the one thing with bullies is that you should never flinch."

The pews included a bipartisan ensemble of the least ordinary men in Australia: Lachlan Murdoch, Frank Lowy, Richard Pratt, Gerry Harvey, Bob

Hawke, Graham Richardson, Andrew Peacock, Jeff Kennett, Peter Costello, Kim Beazley, Kevin Rudd, Richie Benaud, Mark Taylor, Steve Waugh, Ricky Ponting, Greg Norman, Bert Newton, Don Burke and Eddie McGuire.

"The key to the enormous impact he had on the Australian community was his understanding of what made the ordinary bloke tick," Howard told them. "He was a larrikin but he was also a gentleman and that's a dual description that any Australian man would be proud to have."

Language was so hollow in Howard's post-class utopia that a born-to-rule aristocrat and telecommunications tycoon – perhaps the most pathologically materialistic person in Australian public life – could be celebrated as a no-bullshit, down-to-earth, anti-Establishment everyman. Nobody blinked an eye. His qualifications for larrikinism? A love of meat pies and contact sport, along with a chronic gambling addiction.

"He was a sentimental bloke," said Howard, recalling how Packer almost – almost! – shed a tear while watching Makybe Diva win the Cox Plate. "He of course famously loved to bet and he was intensely loyal to his mates."

Malcolm Turnbull's tender republican heart – broken by monarchist Howard – had healed sufficiently for him to become a Liberal backbencher. Now the wannabe king grabbed the microphone. He dedicated an unflinching rendition of "C'Mon Aussie C'Mon" to Kerry Packer. The Sydney Symphony Orchestra played "Waltzing Matilda." A children's choir sang a fitting tribute to the farce of the past decade. Alan Jones got the final word: he invited mourners to the wake for meat pies.

"Nothing could be more KP than a pie," he said.

Nobody mentioned the heaviest elephant in the Opera House that day: Packer's intense melancholia. And why would they? The billionaire's sorrow was the best advertisement for socialism. Phillip Adams later called Australia's richest man the saddest person he'd ever met. Packer once asked Adams – after they negotiated a movie deal at a Chinese restaurant in Kings Cross – for the definition of a black hole. "That's what I've got inside me," said Packer. "A big, black hole." He cut through the spin to the dark heart of the larrikin.

In 2006, Bruce Baird tapped Scott Morrison on the shoulder to replace him as Liberal MP for Cook, the home of *Puberty Blues*, Andrew Ettingshausen and the Cronulla riots. Baird was evidently a man of deep faith: Morrison had been given the flick from the last two government jobs that Baird recommended him for. After leaving Tourism Australia, Morrison oversaw Peter Debnam's disastrous bid to become NSW premier. The trouble wasn't just his patchy work record but winning sympathy from strangers.

The list of personal interests on Morrison's curriculum vitae must have been a red flag for branch members in Cronulla: "Church (Hillsong Church, Waterloo), Family, Politics, Reading (biography, travel, history, Australian fiction), Kayaking, Rugby (Randwick, Waratahs), AFL (Western Bulldogs)."

Unsurprisingly, rugby league wasn't mentioned, because Morrison was a diehard rah-rah who attended the Waratahs' union games at Moore Park. He belonged to a Hillsong congregation in Waterloo, the inner city, where the apocalyptically un-Cronulla Brian Houston was pastor. Morrison became a loyal acolyte of the charismatic Houston, who pumped the spin doctor's tyres up. "Heaven opened over that campus," Houston said later.

First, Morrison needed to win preselection. But little about the Bronte WASP lent itself to humble Cronulla. The Sutherland Shire was the land of the stoned surfer and cashed-up tradie, two constituencies united by Southern Cross tattoos, Such Is Life bumper stickers and cravings for Toohey's New. Morrison was a puritanical apparatchik entering peak Bunnings Warehouse territory without the Trojan horse of a Toyota Hilux.

The local favourite for preselection was a type-A patriot named Michael Towke. *That's not a Howard's Battler*, Towke must've thought when he watched Morrison waltz into the shire from Bronte. *This is a Howard's Battler!*

Towke was the eldest of eight, a Catholic who'd graduated from the macho Marcellin College. At seventeen, he'd joined the Australian Army Reserve. But Towke was no intellectual slouch. He had a first-class honours degree in engineering and a BA from the University of Sydney, where he won the top prize for sociology, followed by an MBA. Much more relevantly for preselection, Morrison's main rival had lived in the Sutherland Shire for the past decade. And he was a devout rugby league fan.

Morrison had the patronage of Baird and a letter of recommendation from the PM. But the spin doctor didn't pass the pub test. The former Liberal state director was knocked out in the first round of the ballot. Towke won 82 to 8. Alas, Towke was Lebanese-Australian. It had been eighteen months since the Cronulla riots. The Liberals were presented with an opportunity to demonstrate that the Sutherland Shire was healing from racial division. That their party was truly a broad church. Instead, they embarked on a vicious smear campaign and factional stitch-up.

"There was a view among some senior Liberals that a Lebanese Australian could not win Cook in a tight election," wrote the *Sydney Morning Herald* journalist Paul Sheehan in 2009.

Michael Towke's character was assassinated via a series of articles in *The Daily Telegraph*. "PM's Candidate Lacks Security," trumpeted the online article above a happy snap of Towke with fiancé Nicole Aghabi, alongside a photo of a dilapidated terrace house in Redfern. It was the apparent address of Towke's small business Apollo Security, which boasted clients such as Pfizer. "This is the type of business Prime Minister John Howard is proud to support," wrote a scornful Simon Benson, who would later become the political editor of *The Australian* and a crucial media ally of Morrison.

The next day, *The Sunday Telegraph* ran the headline "Party Split as Liberal Candidate Faces Jail." Towke claimed the report hospitalised his mother. He was accused of branch stacking and being a Labor mole. According to journalist Deborah Snow, the Liberal Party blackmailed Towke to withdraw and support Morrison. The preselection was held a second time. Morrison duly won. Towke sued News Limited for defamation, negotiating a $50,000 payout. The Liberals secretly reimbursed Towke $30,000 for his legal costs. He had forgotten the golden rule: never let merit get in the way of a GPS boy with mates in high places.

In 2007, Kevin Rudd – the original daggy Christian dad – was sweeping Australian politics thanks to a regular slot on *Sunrise* with Joe Hockey. Rudd was a Mandarin-speaking bureaucrat from rural Queensland, who attended church loyally with wife Therese. His record-breaking approval ratings as Opposition leader seemingly dispelled the myth Australia wouldn't elect a tall poppy as PM. Out of the three previous Labor prime ministers, Rudd had most in common with Whitlam, the big-picture visionary obsessed with education, health care and Asia.

Swinging voters in suburban and regional seats lapped him up precisely because he wasn't a larrikin. They rejected one of their own, Mark Latham, a neoliberal fibro from the western suburbs, who crash-tackled a taxi driver and tried to crush Howard's manhood under his knuckles. Australia was suffering from unprecedented affluence and anxiety. The aspirationals were up to their eyeballs in debt, and heavily reliant on John Howard's middle-class welfare continuing. They'd only be returning to Labor for someone with a safe handshake.

"A number of people have referred to me as an economic conservative," said Rudd in a TV ad. "When it comes to public finance, it's a badge I wear with pride … Some call us the lucky country. But I believe you make your own luck."

Rudd gentrified Howard's tiring paternalism, with more heart on social issues and a bigger role for government on economic ones. He offered an apology to the Stolen Generations, action on climate change to Keating's Elites, plus job security and wage growth to Howard's Battlers. The bedrock of his social program was class solidarity awakened by the "Your Rights at Work" campaign. Labor won twenty-three seats. Fifteen of them were rugby league seats: aspirational electorates in suburban and regional New South Wales and Queensland. A sixteenth, Bennelong, was lost by the sitting PM: John Howard.

"By the time you got to WorkChoices," Rudd tells me, "no amount of green tracksuits, no amount of morning walks, no amount of Canterbury Boys High and Howard's Battler logic could continue to pull the tarpaulin over that ugly piece of furniture left in the middle of the nation's living room."

One of the biggest winners from the Liberals losing government was Scott Morrison, who held Cook, even with a 6.71 per cent swing against him. Howard was gone. Peter Costello and Alexander Downer would follow him out the door. Morrison arrived in Canberra with a reasonable prospect of picking up a shadow ministry and the Liberals not so badly beaten that they couldn't dream of regaining government within one or two terms. Morrison delivered his maiden speech on 14 February 2008. Opposition leader Brendan Nelson sat beside him. Alex Hawke sat over his left shoulder, Peter Dutton over his right. Malcolm Turnbull sat in the front row.

"I like my history in high-definition, widescreen, full, vibrant colour," said Morrison. "There is no doubt that our Indigenous population has been devastated by the inevitable clash of cultures that came with the arrival of the modern world in 1770 at Kurnell in my electorate. This situation is not the result of any one act but of more than 200 years of shared ignorance."

Rhetorically, Scott John Morrison bore little resemblance to ScoMo – the alter ego who hadn't been invented yet. There were no "how goods" and only one "fair go." He made no mention of rugby league or coalmining. The politician in that debut speech was an earnest WASP from the eastern suburbs, who practised the compassionate conservatism of Bruce Baird, not the pitiless wedge politics of John Howard, which seemed obsolete in 2008.

"We are a prosperous people," he declared, "but this prosperity is not solely for our own benefit; it comes with a responsibility to invest."

Morrison was wrongly betting the age of Howardism and Hansonism had ended. This was a pre-GFC world, back in Rudd's shortlived epoch of verbose benevolence. In 2007, a record-breaking 85.6 per cent of Australians expressed trust in democracy. Voters basically believed what politicians were saying to them. Rudd's Newspoll approval hit 71 per cent in August 2008, four points better than Howard's peak and nine points better than Hawke's PB. In 2007, Rudd had declared climate change the great moral challenge of our time. Morrison's rival moral crisis was sub-Saharan hunger. He namedropped Hillsong pastor Brian Houston, along with Desmond Tutu.

"It is a true moral crisis that eclipses all others," said Morrison. "The African tragedy is driven by war, poverty, disease, famine, corruption, injustice and an evil that is robbing generations of Africans, our fellow human beings, of their future … Paul Hewson, better known as Bono, said: 'There is a continent – Africa – being consumed by flames … when the history books are written, our age will be remembered for … what we did – or did not do to put the fire out …'"

The drama-loving chameleon was trying to find the mask that would route him most rapidly to the top. Whereas Rudd advertised himself as John Howard Light to swinging voters, Morrison marketed himself as Kevin Rudd Heavy, an optimistic Christian without the bitter aftertaste of the Labor Party. The humanitarian fire stopped burning for Morrison in September 2008. On 15 September, investment bank Lehman Brothers was placed into liquidation. On 16 September, Malcolm Turnbull won a leadership spill against Brendan Nelson. Morrison was promoted to be the shadow minister for housing and local government.

Overnight, the global financial crisis destroyed the altruistic mood of boom-time Australia. Moralistic politicians offering dreams of a brighter tomorrow became poison among retirees and swinging aspirationals with plunging share and superannuation portfolios. Commodity prices fell by 30 per cent from October 2008 until May 2009, the same drop as the Australian dollar. Miners in Queensland weren't so open-minded about an emissions trading scheme.

"Everyone was all for signing Kyoto," says Lachlan Harris, Rudd's press secretary from 2006 until 2010. "You know why? Because it didn't do anything! We're all gonna get skinny this summer, woohoo! But then it was like: are we really gonna commit to running 10 k's every day? Ah, nah."

Turnbull was the first casualty of the national mood swing. Macho doom-merchant Tony Abbott won the Liberal leadership by a single vote in December 2009 on a platform of climate change denialism. Morrison was promoted to be the shadow minister for immigration. Under pressure from Treasurer Wayne Swan and Deputy Leader Julia Gillard, Rudd put the ETS into the too-hard basket. This precipitated a collapse in his popularity. His government pursued a Resource Super Profit Tax as a makeshift raison d'être.

The RSPT triggered a war with the mining industry. Inspired by Packer and Bond, iron-ore tycoons Gina Rinehart and Andrew "Twiggy" Forrest paraded themselves as dinky-di patriots at a protest in Perth. After a hit from the GFC, Rinehart was worth $4.75 billion and Forrest $4.24 billion. They had a laser-like focus on Howard's Battlers.

"And what are we gonna tell those jittery Labor MPs in marginal seats?" Rinehart asked the crowd, like a house captain at a swimming carnival.

"Axe the tax!" chanted her minions. "Axe the tax!"

"What should our *West Australian* newspaper be saying?" she asked.

"Axe the tax!" they chanted. "Axe the tax!"

The high-visibility tycoons claimed to be motivated not by personal greed but mateship with their working-class employees. They imagined themselves as modern-day Peter Lalors, protesting against an unfair tariff. Abbott's Liberal Party became the political arm of the mining industry, and News Corp the media arm. This was a well-oiled machine. Aristocrats offered higher taxes and action on climate change as a common enemy to battlers.

"I ask you which communist is turning capitalist and which capitalist is turning communist," said a fluorescent Forrest, dressed for a shift in a mining pit in suburban Perth. "We represent the hopes and dreams of thousands and millions of people who depend on the mining industry."

In fact, mining directly employed approximately 133,200 people, or less than 1 per cent of Australia's population. Most of the faux-working-class protestors in Perth were superannuated boomers with too much time on their hands. They waved around identikit placards that had clearly been mass-produced by the mining tycoons. Labor proved incapable of prosecuting modestly populist economic policies without spontaneously self-combusting. Bill Shorten – a Bob Hawke wannabe – conspired with the modern-day Richos in the NSW Right to stage a coup against Rudd, whose support in caucus evaporated.

Julia Gillard – Australia's first female PM – was installed as Rudd's replacement. Historian Clare Wright says that Gillard was a textbook larrikin: the humble roots, the trade union links, the atheism, the childlessness. These are all the hallmarks of a non-conformist thumbing their nose at authority. Journalist Annabel Crabb agrees. She says that Australian politics had a glittering history of "blokes ripping jobs off each other," which wasn't much of a problem until Gillard, and certainly wasn't a problem for Scott Morrison.

"Of all the PMs I've met, I think Gillard and weirdly enough Tony Abbott are the most classic larrikins post-Hawke," says Crabb. "Which is probably why they always got on so well, until they didn't. This easy rapport was often characterised as flirting. Australia can't accommodate two larrikins enjoying each other's company when they don't both have penises."

Julia Gillard and Wayne Swan negotiated a ceasefire with Australia's biggest mining companies and officially kept climate change on the backburner with a citizens' assembly. But Twiggy and Gina were even more furious than before: the deal was with conglomerates such as Rio Tinto and BHP, not them.

Lachlan Harris concedes Rudd was far from perfect, and that staffers like him mismanaged the concerns of caucus. But he believes the spill was ultimately about climate change and the threat to mining, not personality. Rudd restarted a political fight that predated Labor: between free traders and protectionists. University-educated progressives demanded a globally focused, market-based approach to climate change, while the regional working class employed in carbon-exposed industries pleaded for patriotic protectionism.

"Rudd's rise brought that fight to a head," says Harris. "That's what you saw in 2010: the two sides of Whitlam's coalition splitting, and Rudd falling in between them ... His sacking was a decision that cast Labor into the wilderness for a decade. Was he that much of a bastard? Probably not."

*

Tony Abbott offered Fortress Australia to anxious voters and almost brought down a first-term government. Gillard was reduced to minority status. The ALP lost thirteen seats, seven of them in Queensland. Labor's primary vote was cannibalised at both ends of the ideological spectrum. Adam Bandt won the division of Melbourne for the Greens. Labor entered a shotgun marriage with his party, spawning an emissions trading scheme, exactly the kind of policy solution Rudd had been knifed to avoid. Abbott's response was ruthless.

"It wasn't a carbon tax … but we made it a carbon tax," Abbott's chief of staff, Peta Credlin, later admitted. "We made it a fight about the hip pocket and not the environment … That was brutal retail politics and it took Abbott about six months to cut through and when he cut through, Gillard was gone."

The "carbon tax" poured fuel onto the PR inferno lit by the mining industry and drew a nuclear response from News Corp. "Around late 2010, evidence suggests, Rupert Murdoch decided to use his Australian newspapers to destroy the government of Julia Gillard," wrote Robert Manne in *The Monthly*. "As far as I am aware, it was the first such decision with regard to federal Australian politics he had taken since 1975."

Gina Rinehart wanted to decide elections too. She purchased a 10 per cent stake in Network 10, alongside James Packer and Lachlan Murdoch. News Corp opinion columnist Andrew Bolt was given his own TV show. Rinehart also secured a chunk of Fairfax, the main opposition to News Corp's protection racket for mining companies. Hancock Prospecting later increased Rinehart's stake of Fairfax to 18.7 per cent.

"We have been able to overtly and covertly attack governments," John Singleton – a mate of both Rinehart and her father, Lang Hancock – confessed to journalist Jane Cadzow in 2012. "Because we have people employed by us like Andrew Bolt and Alan Jones and Ray Hadley who agree with her thinking about the development of our resources, we act in concert in that way."

Murdoch journalists and right-wing shock jocks collaborated on a sexist character assassination of our first female prime minister. In March 2011, Tony Abbott and Barnaby Joyce spoke at an anti–carbon tax rally outside parliament. Protestors waved placards that read "JuLIAR … BOB BROWNS BITCH" and "DITCH THE WITCH." Abbott and Joyce were both graduates of Riverview, the mind-bogglingly expensive GPS school on Sydney's North Shore. They cloaked their privilege with overblown machismo.

"As I look out on this crowd of fine Australians," said Abbott, beaming at an audience that included Pauline Hanson, whom he had helped to incarcerate, "I want to say that I do not see scientific heretics. I do not see environmental vandals. I see people who want honest government."

In June 2011, Rinehart flew Joyce and Julia Bishop to India on a private jet for the glamorous three-day wedding of G.V. Krishna Reddy's grand-daughter. Rinehart was about to seal a $1-billion deal with Reddy to buy coalmining reserves from Hancock Prospecting. Ten thousand people attended the pumped-up nuptials, including Indian politicians and Bollywood stars. "It was absolutely mind-blowing," Joyce told journalist Katharine Murphy.

Afterwards, a mind-blown Joyce and his wife hitched a lift to Kuala Lumpur by private jet and charged taxpayers $5500 for flights from Malaysia to Australia. In July, Joyce appeared at an anti–carbon tax rally in Sydney. "We are saying this woman and Bob Brown are taking us towards economic suicide," he said. "Julia Gillard will be slaughtered in the next election." The crowd chanted, "Ditch the witch" and "If it's Brown, flush it down."

It was one thing for Howard and Rudd to float an ETS during a boom, and for Abbott to support one after the bust, and another for a carbon tax to come from Gillard and Brown during a new boom. Hanson's popularity was burgeoning among the same apoplectic voters staging public protests against Gillard, fed by the homicidal vitriol of Alan Jones.

"The woman's off her tree and quite frankly they should shove her and Bob Brown in a chaff bag and take them as far out to sea as they can and tell them to swim home," said Jones, shortly after Joyce's calls for slaughter.

Whereas the billionaires and shock jocks offered idolisation to miners, Gillard and Brown provided tough love. But the blokes populating mine sites weren't going to have their high-risk jobs – and heavily leveraged lifestyles – threatened by a woman from Victoria and a gay man from Tasmania. The "carbon tax" solidified the coalition between blue-collar swagmen and the posh squatters responsible for their stagnating wages. Rinehart – a wannabe bush poet – composed an elegy for egalitarianism.

"Is our future threatened with massive debts run up by political hacks," she wrote, blending Ayn Rand and Banjo Paterson. "Who dig themselves out by unleashing rampant tax … The world's poor need our resources: do not leave them to their fate. Our nation needs special economic zones and wise government, before it is too late."

In 2012, the poem was etched into a thirty-tonne iron-ore boulder outside a shopping centre in suburban Perth. The boom was back, baby! According to *Forbes*, Gina Rinehart was the twenty-ninth richest person in the world, three spots shy of Jeff Bezos. The BRW Rich List estimated Rinehart's net worth at $29.17 billion.

According to Andrew Leigh's book *Battlers and Billionaires*, Australia's level of inequality hit a seventy-year low in 1980. The top 1 per cent's share of household income sat at 5 per cent, while the top 0.01 per cent's share sat at 1 per cent. By 2010, the top 1 per cent's share of the national income had almost doubled, to 9 per cent. The top 0.01 per cent's share of the national income had tripled, to 3 per cent. This represented a $403-billion redistribution from the bottom 99 per cent to the top 1 per cent.

"Just as the top is accelerating away from the middle, so too has the bottom fallen away from the middle," wrote Leigh, who was elected as a federal Labor MP in 2010. "If you think of inequality as being like a foot race, everyone is still moving in the same direction, but the front runners are accelerating away from the pack, while the laggards are falling further behind."

Scott Morrison took notes as Abbott's monosyllabic slogans destroyed the prime ministership of a Christian bureaucrat. Desmond Tutu went out the window. In December 2010, an Indonesian fishing boat carrying eighty-nine asylum seekers and three crew members smashed against the rocks of Christmas Island. Fifty of them drowned in the Indian Ocean. Morrison criticised the Gillard government for flying bereaved relatives to the funerals in Sydney. It was enough to make Joe Hockey and even Tony Abbott blush.

"I'm very disappointed that Scott would make those comments," said Bruce Baird, perhaps realising that his protégé had been irretrievably recruited to the far, far dark side of the Liberal Party. "It is lacking in compassion at the very time when these people have been through such a traumatic event."

The Bono-quoting bleeding heart had been replaced by a right-wing Rottweiler. According to journalist Lenore Taylor, Morrison pushed cabinet to capitalise on Islamophobia. The ScoMo persona was a work in progress. Morrison had grasped the electoral importance of loathing boat people, but not yet of loving the Cronulla Sharks. His new local team had been on the brink of extinction since inception. Jack Gibson – the greatest coach of all time – famously said that waiting for Cronulla to win a premiership was like leaving the porch light on for Harold Holt.

The scene was set for Morrison's road to Damascus moment. He bought a family home in Cronulla. The long-suffering Sharks ran equal first. But the new local member stayed meticulously indifferent to rugby league. "why the dogs and not the swans," he tweeted in 2009. "because rodney eade sparked my interest in the great game #afl and loyalty counts." Scotty from Bronte was leaving a trail of breadcrumbs should he hypothetically require the swinging voters of Victoria to clinch power.

"I'm more of a rugby fan," Morrison confessed on Twitter in 2010, "but naturally when it comes to the NRL, the Sharks have my loyalty."

Before the 2013 election, Labor resurrected KRudd at the last minute to save the furniture. His most loyal supporter in cabinet was Anthony Albanese. Albo didn't look or speak like Labor's new breed of MPs. He was a working-class rugby league nut with a beer gut, crooked teeth, a bad wardrobe and rough communication style. He trimmed the eyebrows, bought some new ties and received dental attention. But he was still a breath of fresh air compared to the slick apparatchiks who blew up the ALP. Rudd made him deputy prime minister.

"I am from a rural working-class background," Rudd tells me. "I went to a state primary school and a state high school. My ability to make the most of my life was underpinned by a federal Labor government giving me a free education. End of story. When I look at Albo and the reality of his upbringing, it's not dissimilar, frankly, apart from the fact that he wasn't on a farm."

Nonetheless, Labor lost in a landslide. Abbott's Coalition won eighteen seats and 53.49 per cent of the two-party-preferred vote. Rudd stood down. Albanese ran for the leadership of the Labor Party. He comfortably won the vote of grassroots ALP members, but was unable to win over enough MPs. Instead, they chose Bill Shorten, the public face of Labor's malaise.

Morrison emerged as the best performer in the Abbott government. He initiated Operation Sovereign Borders, an authoritarian war on boat people that claimed credit for punitive measures introduced by Rudd and Albanese. The immigration minister kept a trophy on his desk in the shape of an Indonesian fishing boat, engraved with a monosyllabic catchphrase: I Stopped These.

"There's a deep insecurity at the heart of Australia," says Omar Sakr. "We all know that it's stolen land … Which leads to the ridiculous branding of Fortress Australia and Sovereign Borders. It's predicated on the terror that what white Australians did to the Indigenous people will be done to them."

Seeking reinvention, Morrison traded immigration for social services and cultivated a more laidback image. Being a head-kicker didn't make swinging voters in New South Wales and Queensland want to have a beer with him. In 2015, Abbott was replaced by Malcolm Turnbull, who promised a softer touch. Morrison became treasurer. The opposing leaders at the 2016 election exuded the desire to be admired as smart by the media class. Turnbull won the election as unconvincingly as Shorten attacked a democracy sausage. The unexpected closeness cloaked the aversion for Shorten. Albo decided not to challenge for the Labor leadership.

2016 was a sliding doors moment for Western civilisation generally, and Morrison specifically. The treasurer was heir apparent to Turnbull. But he detected a scarcity of retail politicians, and officially defected from rugby union to the People's Republic of Rugby League. The member for Cook became the number-one ticket holder of the Cronulla Sharks. This epitomised the unlikely romance between rugby league and the conservative elite that had spent roughly a hundred years attempting to crush it. Aussie Rules was as beloved by bankers in Kooyong and hipsters in Fitzroy as it was by bogans in Bendigo. At a Sharks game, Morrison was a big fish in a small pond, which matched the parochial mood of the geopolitical moment.

"I was one of the very few Libs who played rugby league before I knew anything about politics, and who kept watching after my career ended," John Fahey told me in 2020. "Morrison was a rugby union fan. But he realised that rugby league has everything to do with the white picket fence suburbs, as Howard called them."

Morrison's timing was impeccable. In 2016, Cronulla Sharks won their first premiership. "All to play for," Morrison tweeted with a selfie alongside Howard and Turnbull. "Cronulla Sharks getting weighty support." Morrison belonged to a rich history of class cross-dressers at Sydney rugby league stadiums. Roy Masters – who started the great class war between the fibros and silvertails – later confessed that he inspired plenty of pretenders.

"Wests fans began to dress down for games and became curiously quiet if they lived in a bluestone house in Strathfield," he wrote for the Tom Brock Lecture. "I knew a pharmacist from Ashfield who left his chemist shop at noon on Saturdays, drove home, took off his coat and tie, wore a boilersuit to Lidcombe and carried two narrow slats of fibro, nailed at the bottom of one end. He stood on the hill … opening them to a V when we scored a try."

Like the Ashfield chemist in a boilersuit at Lidcombe Oval, Morrison cycled through working-class costumes while banging rhetorical slats of fibro together so that the angry mob identified him as an ally, not a rat. In January 2017, shock jock Ray Hadley noticed that the hi-vis treasurer had added a DIY nickname – ScoMo – in brackets to his Facebook profile. The last political leader to be known so casually by a nickname was Hawkey.

"So you're on Facebook now as … ScoMo," said Hadley.

"That's how people are increasingly getting to know me," said ScoMo.

A month later, Morrison smuggled a lump of coal into Question Time. He was signalling unambiguously to blue-collar battlers in regional Australia – along with white-collar reactionaries on the Coalition back-bench and in the boardrooms of mining companies – that he'd fight for "real jobs" against the snobs sitting opposite and also beside him.

"This is coal," he barked. "Don't be afraid! Don't be scared!"

ScoMo was a manifesto in perpetual motion. A bloke drinking a beer in a Cronulla Sharks jersey doesn't need to tell you that political correctness has gone mad. And someone who juggles a lump of coal in Question Time doesn't need to call global warming a hoax. The treasurer was Hemingway-esque when it came to showing rather than telling. The images did all the heavy lifting necessary in Maitland and Mackay, while maintaining plausible deniability in Bondi and Brighton that he wasn't a full-blown climate change denier. The genius of Morrison's new persona was that unlike Trump or Johnson, he didn't even need to offer concrete policies that challenged the neoliberal consensus in Australian politics. ScoMo was a vibe.

"It's coal!" he roared, after offloading the rock to Barnaby Joyce, like a prop to a playmaker. "It was dug up by men and women who work and live in the electorates of those who sit opposite, from the Hunter Valley … There's no word for coal-o-phobia, Mr Speaker, but that's the malady that afflicts those opposite!"

Scotty from Marketing was the suburban version of Barnaby Joyce. Barn cosplayed as a god-fearing farmer, who opposed abortion, gay marriage and Chinese communists, while rooting staffers and cosying up to mining tycoons. But Joyce was plagued by the occupational hazards of being a fair dinkum larrikin. In February 2018, News Corp revealed that the married father of four was expecting a child with ex–press secretary Vikki Campion. He left his wife, but not before questioning the paternity of Campion's baby. Turnbull put Barnaby on gardening duties and introduced a "Bonk Ban" to parliament.

The career of the deputy prime minister seemed at little risk until Catherine Marriott – a former WA Rural Woman of the Year – revealed that the Nationals had botched her accusations of sexual harassment against him. Joyce reluctantly quit for the backbench. He sharpened a hatchet for the climate change policies of the holier-than-thou PM, aiming to do to Turnbull's National Energy Guarantee what he did to Gillard's carbon tax. "We are sick of having all these caveats placed on us by green groups, by well-intentioned, well-paid people in Giorgio Armani suits, sitting back and pontificating about the world, and then leaving the bill," said Joyce.

Within a month, Turnbull was mugged from the front by Abbott and Joyce, cheered on by Jones and Bolt. Peter Dutton was the preferred PM of Rupert Murdoch, but "Dutto" didn't have the same ring to it. ScoMo presented himself as the most likeable lunatic in the asylum. His Pentecostal supporters rigged the numbers, knifing Turnbull from behind and leapfrogging Dutton and foreign minister Julie Bishop to the throne. Turnbull was the third prime minister in eight years burnt at the stake by climate change.

"The National Energy Guarantee was a coherent integration of climate and energy policy," tweeted Turnbull after leaving politics. "It was sabotaged by the right wing of the coalition and their supporters in the media and coal lobby and finally abandoned by Morrison Government."

On 24 August, Morrison emerged from the coup as the compromise candidate. "Everyman-makes-it-to-PM type of deal," Bruce Baird – a career politician with a tenuous grasp of the idea of an everyman – told commentator Sean Kelly.

ScoMo resembled a stunned mullet. It was as if he'd accidentally stumbled into the press conference at Parliament House from Shark Park, and not spent the last decade obsessively reinventing himself to become the prime minister. He made the most of the unexpected turn of events, and negotiated a verbal Fair Go Agreement with the equally dumbfounded electorate. "If you have a go in this country, you'll get a go," he declared. "There's a fair go for those who have a go … We have come to have a go. And we will get a fair go."

The lucky country was run by a plucky everyman, as if Forrest Gump were a Cronulla Sharks fan, but with none of the friendly intentions. There was no time for idle chitchat about Bono, Desmond Tutu and Brian Houston. "We all want to be able to make our own choices in life," he said. "Whether it is about who comes to our country, as John Howard famously said … or what team they want to follow. I suggest the Sharks."

In lieu of new policy ideas, ScoMo sprinkled Hawke's ocker common touch on the base of Howard's suburban conservatism, producing the perfect mishmash of a mate and a dad. He evoked a distant era when prime ministers lasted longer than a home reno. Highbrow listeners cringed at the slow cadences of Morrison's larrikin aphorisms. The references to sport were Hawke-like in their gratuitousness. But they were music to the ears of voters like my brother John, who belongs to a far vaster constituency than intellectuals.

"Abbott was too opinionated," says John. "Turnbull spoke in riddles. ScoMo talks like a normal bloke. He reminds me of Bob Hawke."

One surprising source of admiration for the prime minister's communication skills is Greens senator Lidia Thorpe. Thorpe – a proud Gunnai Gunditjmara and Djab Wurrung woman – comes from an economically disadvantaged background. She has studied Morrison's clarity in the flesh and found him utterly convincing, even when she vehemently disagrees with the sentiments expressed. Thorpe believes progressives need to meet people on their level and get better at connecting with voters who don't have university degrees. "The prime minister is very good with his marketing," she says. "He comes into your lounge room and he's your mate. And it works very well. His articulation of the issues is very clear … People have got to like you."

*

In the week following the Libspill – and all the way to the 2019 election – Morrison's two-year-old infatuation with the Sharks became the defining feature of his existence. There was strategy behind this.

The deputy campaign director of the Liberal Party was Isaac Levido, a protégé of Sir Lynton Crosby, the architect of Howard's dog-whistle strategy in 1996. Levido was born in the Hunter Valley. His grandfather and uncles played for the Cessnock Goannas, a rugby league team in coal country that produced Matthew and Andrew Johns. Andrew Johns is regarded as the greatest rugby league player of all time. His dad, Gary, was a third-generation coalminer who captain-coached the Goannas. "Growing up in Cessnock," Andrew Johns told radio host Richard Fidler in 2009, "all we wanted to do was play rugby league for Cessnock and work in the coal mines."

Levido knew intuitively what would appeal to voters in regional New South Wales and Queensland: coal, rugby league and golden ale. A month after promotion, ScoMo bragged to Matty Johns on Triple M's *The Grill Team* about telling Eddie McGuire he doesn't rate Aussie Rules, airbrushing any affinity for the Western Bulldogs.

"What's your biggest vice, Prime Minister?" asked the host.

"I like a beer," said the copper's son, who wasn't allowed to join the surf club due to his father's fear of a sherbet.

It is nothing new for ambitious politicians to partake in the hobbies of the great unwashed for photo ops, or to jump on the bandwagon of a successful sporting team. But it takes an innovative shamelessness to drop compulsive references to beer and the Sharks even privately among old acquaintances who know you are full of shit. The equivalent would be if Paul Keating had started bull-frogging VBs and belting out "Good Old Collingwood Forever" at the parliament bar in the lead-up to knifing

Hawke, or if Peter Costello had nicknamed himself "Cozza" and started talking like Steve Irwin after the 2004 election. Morrison was pretending to be someone who wasn't pretending to be someone that he wasn't – and doing an extremely professional job of it.

"I don't have an Akubra, mate," ScoMo told farmers before embarking on a tour of drought-stricken Queensland. "So I'm just going to bring my Sharks hat … [I'm] not pretending to know one end of a sheep from another."

The PM was widely pilloried for the ScoMobile, a bus that travelled along the coast of Queensland through places like Bundaberg. The beer-gutted Morrison gobbled down garden-variety meat pies like a hungover brick-layer on a five-minute lunch break. He wanted swinging voters to see him as an easygoing slob, not an elitist obsessed with vocabulary, BMI and social status. The prime minister's 100 per cent lack of intellectual superiority and physical perfectionism was a drug to parochials like my brother John.

"It's very tiring to constantly get the message there's something wrong with your lifestyle," says John. "Every human being just wants to be respected. So when you come across someone who doesn't judge how you look or talk – and who doesn't care if you have a university degree – it's deadset one of the nicest feelings in the world."

Morrison turned the 2019 election into a referendum on who you would rather have a beer with. On paper, no other Labor leader had been more similar to Hawke than Bill Shorten. Australia's most famous faceless man worked at a butcher's shop while studying law at Monash University, and later served in the Australian Army Reserve. He cut his teeth in the hyper-masculine trade union movement. Like Hawke, he rose to prominence outside parliament, partly through the Beaconsfield mine disaster, a per-formance that endeared him to the battlers trapped inside a collapsed shaft, and the ones watching breakfast TV. He retained a reputation for being able to sweep businesspeople – and women – off their feet, à la Hawke. Shorten – missing wharfie dad, single mum – had an even better battler yarn to spin than Hawke. Bill should've been an olive branch to Labor's mythical base.

Unfortunately, elections aren't won or lost on paper, but in the split-second impressions of whimsical swinging voters, who pay no attention to the biographies of politicians. Exactly the same people who you'd imagine might be attracted to Shorten's story of humble beginnings – and economic policies that tangibly benefited their families – shared Facebook memes about him being a criminal and a wimp. My brother John was one of them.

"Mate, there are two types of people who Australians don't like: know-it-alls and smart-arses," says John. "And Bill Shorten was both."

Whereas Hawke was seen as a statesman, voters regarded Shorten as a backstabber. Hawke was a people person. Shorten was called a try-hard or a social butterfly. Hawke was one of the boys. Shorten wore a shirt that said "Vote 1: Chloe Shorten's Husband." In 2017, it took him an excruciating sixteen seconds to drink 425 millilitres. Hawke could sink three schooners in the same time at the age of eighty-seven.

On the Friday night before the election, John posted a YouTube video of Hawkey skulling a beer, and toasted his memory with a XXXX Gold. The next day, he voted for Hawke's spiritual son: ScoMo, not Shorten. This played out across the country. Cosmopolitans voted for redistribution and action on climate change. But the target audience for Labor's policies in suburban and regional seats swung towards the Coalition. Parochials like John voted for the trickle-down effect.

According to the ANU Australian Election Study, Morrison was the most popular major-party candidate at a federal election since Rudd in 2007. Shorten was the least popular since Andrew Peacock in 1990. Geoff Cousins had the advertising account for the Liberals at the 1990 election. "Andrew Peacock was a delightful person," Cousins tells me. "Australians said they thought that he was a terrific bloke. He takes out Shirley MacLaine. They'd love to have a beer with him at the races. But he doesn't seem a person of sufficient weight. Whereas Hawkey was a larrikin. But he's very smart, and he fights for things."

Cousins argues Hawke and Howard were united by a willingness to fight their own base: Hawke for the deregulation of the economy, Howard against guns and for the GST. After a distinguished career in business and acting as an adviser to Howard, Cousins became an unlikely environmental warrior, waging war against the Gunns paper mill in Tasmania. And he believes that Morrison didn't win the last election; Shorten lost it.

"Shorten assured me in very specific terms that he was going to formulate a strong policy on Adani," says Cousins. "I asked him what would happen if he received opposition from his own party. He said, 'I'm going to stare them down.' Well, that lasted about fourteen days. That's why he lost. Australians are pretty darn good at picking up weakness."

Labor was fighting a class war on three fronts – against the Liberal Party, News Corp, and mining tycoons – without a propaganda machine or an army of rusted-on voters. A confederacy of squatters and shock jocks offered belonging and self-esteem to demoralised parochials, without the wage increases or better services enabled by the labour movement. The cosmopolitans generally surrendered. Most of them had no capacity – or burning desire – to build a movement of human beings with contradictory beliefs and disparate postcodes.

"The punditry get sucked into their own groupthink," says Terri Butler, who replaced Rudd as the ALP's member for Griffith in 2014. "They've all known each other for years. But very few of them know what it's like to live in the outer suburbs of Brisbane, or in Townsville … They have private health insurance. Their kids go to private schools. And they know that they've got social connections to get their kids a great start in life."

The terrible truth is that the cosmopolitans can afford to lose. Many make a living from faking outrage at the Establishment that by and large they belong to. The right do whatever is necessary to gain and hold power, while the left prefer virtuous defeats to imperfect victories.

When Scott Morrison reinvented himself as Australia's most passionate rugby league fan and smuggled a lump of coal into parliament, electorates like Capricornia in Central Queensland were at the heart of his PR strategy.

Labor has held Capricornia for roughly three-quarters of the time since Federation, and the state seat of Rockhampton for most of the past century. Voters here are receptive to egalitarian economic policies. But they are extremely reliant on the use of fossil fuels. According to the 2016 census, 11 per cent of the adults in Capricornia are employed by coalmining, the most of any seat in the country.

In 2019, I interviewed an anti-Adani cattle farmer named John Burnett, whose family has lived near Clermont, in Capricornia, for more than a century. "There's two Labor parties," he told me. "The old blue-collar Labor, which a lot of miners relate to and a lot of rural people like me can sympathise with. But the bloody solicitor-driven, yuppie, white-collar Labor that's running the party now doesn't reflect the views of this part of the world any more than the silver-spoon Liberals do."

Michelle Landry narrowly won Capricornia for the LNP at the 2013 election. In 2019, Labor tried to win it back by preselecting a larrikin. Russell Robertson is built like a brick shithouse and has a goatee, but is more softly spoken than you might imagine, because he clearly doesn't need to prove his blokiness. "Robbo" works 120 metres below ground level in an open-cut coalmine, like his father, grandfather and great-grandfather before him. Robertson's mum was a nurse. Both his parents were union members and served as officials in their local Labor branch in Clermont. He has had a gutful of people attacking the party for preselecting miners.

"The Labor Party was founded in Queensland by striking sheep shearers," says Robertson. "I work with my hands every day. You don't get more working-class than that. I am quintessentially Labor. Someone hiding out and blaming coalminers is not the Labor Party."

The 2019 election was dominated by the debate about the proposed Adani coalmine. Bill Shorten was wedged by environmental activists on the left and climate-change deniers on the right. The defining moment happened in Robbo's hometown of Clermont. Bob Brown's convoy of cosmopolitans was met with open hostility from pro-Adani parochials, including Labor's candidate for Capricornia.

According to the 2016 census, Australia has five seats where coal is the biggest job provider: Flynn, Capricornia and Dawson in Queensland, and Hunter and Paterson in New South Wales. In those seats, 10.86 per cent of adults have a university degree and 41.68 per cent are employed in blue-collar industries. In 2007, Rudd won Dawson, Capricornia, Flynn, Paterson and Hunter while offering an ETS. In 2019, Shorten got hammered. Across the five coalmining seats, the average primary vote for populist right-wing parties was 23.23 per cent. Traditional Labor voters sought protection from Hanson, Palmer and Katter, and almost all of their preferences went back to the Coalition.

"The Greens divided Labor from the working class," says Robertson. "It was a disaster in Central Queensland. They didn't stop a project or slow the industry down. All they did was stop Labor from winning government."

This would be easy to dismiss as a coalminer protecting his own neck. And it would be foolish for Labor to build the entire party around appeasing such a small section of the national electorate. More broadly, Australia needs to develop a modernised and gender-neutral understanding of class. We have barely moved past the archetype of Jimmy Barnes's "Working Class Man." The female kindergarten assistant earning $50,000 a year to raise other people's kids doesn't fit our traditional idea of a working-class battler. Whereas a hi-vis, Liberal-voting miner earning a six-figure income for twenty years – and with the property and share portfolios to show for it – can play the class card at the slightest hint of redistribution.

"I wish politicians would stop talking so much about tradies and miners," says Bruce, an electrician on a gas mine. "Some of us blokes are on a coupla hundred grand. We're doing just fine. When was the last time you heard any politicians kick up a stink about the single mum cleaning the shitters at a nursing home? Or the bloke delivering Uber Eats on a bicycle for $5 a pop. That's the real working class, mate."

But Russell Robertson's point about class shouldn't be entirely disregarded, either. The class rebellion against Labor is much more widespread than male coalminers in Central Queensland. At the 2019 federal election, working mums in suburban Victoria swung to the Coalition by twelve points from the 2018 state election. Morrison seemed more humble and trustworthy to a range of voters. Why? My brother John lives in the seat of Hinkler, south of Flynn. According to the 2016 census, 9.7 per cent of adults there have a degree, whereas 38 per cent of adults are blue collar. Nobody in John's social circle attended university. His best mates are self-employed tradies.

"People ask: *where do your kids go to school? Oh, really, the public one,*" says John. "Like they're better than them. Mate, I could afford private school for the girls. It'd be tight. But I want them to know it's not the school you go to that makes you successful in life. Just hard work and being a good person."

John's hard-knock background doesn't make his views more inherently valuable than those of a doctor's son born in Mosman. I disagree with him on a range of issues, especially climate change, and I don't think that Labor should chase his vote in a race to the bottom. But the contempt he feels emanating from progressives isn't an anecdotal anomaly. The brutal reality is that there are a whole lot of Johns across Australia, and indeed the rest of Western civilisation. Every three years, John gets the chance to prove that his opinion has equal weight to those of our university-educated brother and sister, who vote for the Greens.

"Labor became a party for people who went to uni," says John. "As people get more educated, they get more opinionated. But even if what you're saying is factually true, it doesn't mean that I need to agree with you."

In *Capital and Ideology*, Thomas Piketty catalogued the migration of white-collar voters from right-wing parties to left-wing ones, and the exodus of blue-collar ones to the right, culminating overseas in the triumph of Trump and Brexit. Data provided to *The Australian* from Piketty's next book showed that 65.9 per cent of Labor voters identified as working class in 1972, compared to 35 per cent in 2019. In 1972, 57.1 per cent of Liberal voters identified as upper or middle class, compared to 31.6 per cent in 2019. In 1963, just 19.5 per cent of Labor voters had university degrees, compared to 63.1 per cent of Liberals. By 2019, 37 per cent of Labor voters had university degrees, compared to 24.3 per cent of Liberals.

"Labor lost support amongst its traditional base of lower-income working people," said the ALP report into the 2019 defeat. "Economically vulnerable workers living in outer-metropolitan, regional and rural Australia have lost trust in politicians and political institutions … They are the same demographic that swung against the Democrats towards Donald Trump in 2016 and who are ditching progressive parties around the western world."

At the 2019 election, Labor attracted an average swing of 3.78 per cent in the twenty seats with the highest percentage of university graduates. In the twenty seats with the lowest percentage of university graduates, Labor suffered an average 4.22 per cent swing against it. This was a reversal of the 2016 election, when Turnbull gained ground in affluent electorates and Shorten in working-class ones. The Coalition was aided by Murdoch buying all of the newspapers in regional Queensland and mining tycoon Clive Palmer flooding their front pages with pro-Adani propaganda. But Morrison crystallised a philosophical difference between the Coalition and Labor on blue-collar jobs in a way the urbane Turnbull couldn't.

On election night, ScoMo attributed the shock victory to divine intervention. "I have always believed in miracles," he said. "How good is Australia? And how good are Australians? They have their dreams … To get a job. To get an apprenticeship. To start a business. To meet someone amazing."

ScoMo was Australia's larrikin messiah, leading aspirational battlers in regional Queensland to the Promised Land of tax cuts for the North Shore and soaring profits for mining tycoons. The day after the election, Morrison went to his Pentecostal church in the Sutherland Shire – Horizon – followed by a visit to Cronulla's real cathedral: Shark Park. In front of 13,360 people, the Sharks lost 24–14 to the Manly Sea Eagles. On the news, casual bystanders couldn't tell that Cronulla had been beaten from the vision of the PM helicoptering a Sharks scarf above his Sharks cap with an obligatory schooner of beer, like Cronulla had just won the grand final.

"I don't see Scott Morrison as having any of the qualities of the lovable larrikin," says Geoff Cousins. "He's what we call a wowser, who just pretends to be one of the boys."

Like Paul Hogan's Mick Dundee, Scott Morrison's ScoMo alter ego was a big swinging shtick. He mimicked the ocker accent and macho bravura of the Aussie larrikin, without any legitimate commitment to egalitarianism. The 2019 election result was so workmanlike that the Liberal Party exported the game plan to the Tories in England. Isaac Levido was recruited to be the head honcho for Boris Johnson's re-election attempt. Westminster was a hell of a long way from Cessnock. But the north of England was basically the Hunter Valley.

A right-wing think tank gave Johnson's target voter a name: the Workington Man. Workington is an old coalmining town in northern England that has always voted Labour. The Workington Man was a male over the age of forty with no degree, who was pro-rugby league and anti–European Union. It was a British iteration of the Howard Battler. Levido was so successful at recruiting the Workington Man for BoJo that Conservative Party staffers chanted his name on election night, as a swathe of rugby league seats in Labour's "Red Wall" fell to the Tories.

"It's not always the people who say the most who need to be heard," says John. "It's the people who say the least. That's why you have silent voters. We've seen elections in a lot of different countries which didn't go the way people who supposedly know everything said they should've gone. We're not gonna tell you what we're gonna do. But you'll see what happens in the wash."

Russell Robertson is a real-life version of the Workington Man. He hasn't switched to the Tories or succumbed to nihilism. He is running for the ALP again at the 2022 election. After thirteen-hour shifts in a coalmining pit, Robbo sacrifices precious time with his wife and kids to travel vast distances across Queensland between community events. He is sick of left-wing activists attacking his identity and right-wing charlatans plagiarising it.

"Matt Canavan changed his social media profile to make it look like he's just walked out of an underground mine," says Robertson. "This is a guy with an economics degree, whose first job was as a political staffer."

The Coalition is filled with bullshit artists dressed in coalface, the class equivalent of blackface. It is easy to laugh at the shamelessness, and harder to counter it. If Labor doesn't stem the flow of voters in coalmining communities, it will almost certainly lose Hunter and Paterson at the next election, and possibly Shortland. This is why a hysterical Joel Fitzgibbon has spent the last two years banging slats of fibro together in hi-vis vests.

The answer of many cosmopolitans is to let the Coalition have regional Queensland and the Hunter Valley. This would farewell eight seats that have recently elected Labor candidates, including three traditionally safe seats in the Hunter Valley that Labor currently holds.

Terri Butler attended Cairns State High. She was the first member of her family to finish high school and did most of her degree at James Cook University in Townsville. Some of her cousins in North Queensland are the target audience for One Nation: most didn't get degrees or high-paying jobs and have no residual gratitude for Labor's higher education reforms. Their lives range from "just tough" to "really fucking tough."

"It's weird achieving social mobility in your own lifetime," Butler tells me. "Working-class people don't see you as working class. Middle-class people look down on you because of the way you talk or the school you went to."

Butler witnessed her father get made redundant while working at Australia Post. Her mother got made redundant by the Newman government while employed as a teacher's aide. Her dad now works as a wardsperson in a public hospital, and her mum part-time at a public school. She joined the Left faction of the Australian Labor Party to stand up for people like them.

"Imagine having a life where you can't tell the difference between the Liberal Party and the Labor Party," says Butler. "It matters to my family whether or not Labor is in power. It matters whether public health is good or bad, and whether public schools are great or shit."

After the shock election loss, Butler was promoted to the shadow environment ministry. She attended an inner-city dinner party in Sydney with academics. A distinguished professor told Butler that "everyone agreed" the ALP should declare the death of fossil fuels if it was elected, despite the vehement disagreement about action on climate change destroying Labor for the past decade. "That might be what her and all her friends think," Butler tells me. "But say that on the main streets of Rockhampton and see how people react. She said: 'Don't you see that having more radical climate change policies would bring you so many new seats?' And I said: 'Well, name them.' And she couldn't name any."

A bunch of people I have interviewed since the 2019 election claim that Shorten would have won if he had totally opposed Adani and offered a fast-tracked transition. This is a tantalising alternative history for people like me, who believe in the urgent need for climate-change action and who won't be hugely affected by the shift. Unfortunately, I'm not sure it's that simple. The thesis assumes a critical mass of Coalition voters who are so passionate about climate change that they would've switched to Labor if Bill Shorten adopted a hardline position on Adani. But because Shorten vacillated, they stayed with the guy who smuggled a lump of coal into Question Time and who said during the election campaign that electric cars would be the death of the weekend.

Passivity towards climate change isn't a working-class problem, monopolised by uneducated rednecks. At the 2016 census, Australia's five most educated electorates were North Sydney, Bradfield, Wentworth, Kooyong and Higgins. Demographically, they are the mirror opposite of the coalmining seats: 47.42 per cent of adults have a degree; only 10.52 per cent of adults are employed in blue-collar industries. And yet Australia's least blue-collar seats elected the party of climate-change denial, because they hate the redistribution of wealth more than they want to reduce carbon emissions.

If the affluent electorates filled with small-l Liberals were waiting for Labor to oppose Adani before switching over, why didn't they elect Greens candidates, a party stuck on 10 per cent of the vote for most of the past decade? It's a moot point now. But Shorten promising to kill coalmining probably would have produced a more pronounced version of the ultimate election result: Labor getting a bigger swing towards it in seats it has never won, and a bigger swing against it in seats that it holds or is capable of winning.

"Labor could be the ideal party for people who aren't voting on material grounds," says Butler. "And we'd be hopelessly destined to stay in opposition forever."

Labor has made the hardheaded decision that the only path to victory is building a patchwork electoral coalition of cosmopolitans and parochials, and attempting to make action on climate change palatable to battlers. Someone like Robbo could be a circuit-breaker in Central Queensland. He has more in common philosophically with Joel Fitzgibbon and Matt Canavan than with Bob Brown, and wants an open debate with those who wish that all coalmines were shut down yesterday. But he also accepts the transition to renewables and wants Labor to be in charge of it.

"I don't think that people in the southern states have put any thought into how you create renewables," says Robertson. "It's going to be based around mining. Whether you're going to mine rare earth metals for smart devices, coking coal for steel production, bauxite for the aluminium."

How *do* you build a wind turbine without steel? It is the sort of question that doesn't get much airtime at writers' festivals. Robbo is trying to win the battlers of Capricornia back by declaring class war on limp-wristed cosmopolitans with a familial connection to the proletariat, such as me. "The first thing these people will claim is: 'my father was' and 'my family is,'" says Robertson. "*We* are working-class. *We* are in the regions. *We* do the heavy lifting ... If inner-city Labor can't relate to the hardworking coalminer, then we are doomed to a conservative government for a lot longer."

*

A few weeks before he suffered a fatal stroke, I visited my father at the three-star motel he was leasing in Bundaberg. It was the end of winter 2011. Business had been booming since the summer floods. Dad had lifted the occupancy rates of a basket case from 20 per cent to 80 per cent. At the age of sixty-two, he worked roughly ten hours most days, seven days a week. Insanely, he washed the sheets, pillowcases and towels himself, rather than outsourcing the job to a laundromat. This level of workaholism was terrible for his life expectancy and promising for me getting an early inheritance.

"Chicken is for women," my father – who ate red meat every day of his adult life – told me when I was a little kid. "Fish is for Christians."

That morning, I had taken the five-hour train ride from Brisbane to Bundaberg. The Sundowner was populated by the battlers I rarely came across in daily life. I was studying political science and literature at the University of Queensland, a handsome sandstone campus. After a nervous breakdown in the first year of university, I was achieving straight high distinctions and starting to think that perhaps my boyhood political ambitions weren't dead, buried and cremated after all. I might not become the prime minister, but maybe I could be speechwriter for one, or write about them for a living.

I was a young man suffocating from class-consciousness. My mum was from the welfare class. My dad was from the working class. My siblings were from the underclass. My parents gradually escaped the bottom tax bracket. By the time I started primary school, they owned a small business and investment properties. But unlike me, they were incapable of assimilating into the middle class. "Your parents are bogans," a classmate at my Catholic private school told me in Grade Eight, the closest that I've ever come to punching someone.

"Talk about bogans is a way for elites to talk about working class (usually but not always white) people as though they were an inferior species," wrote David Nichols in *The Bogan Delusion*.

Throughout my teens, I internalised all of the bigoted comments about bogans and bludgers, and regurgitated them, even though I was guilty of denigrating people with similar speaking styles and appearances to members of my own family. My parents didn't adhere to the standards of sophistication that I absorbed by religiously watching the ABC. My single mum had spent time in psychiatric wards and was now on the Disability Support Pension. My brother Trent was an unemployed single dad, who'd spent time in prison. He was covered with tattoos and had a front tooth blackened from a fight. My sister Rebecca dropped out of school at the end of Grade Ten to work as a cleaner, and fell pregnant to the son of a meat-worker by the age of sixteen.

I kept these facts a secret from my middle- and upper-class friends at university. In the big smoke, I changed my speaking style and developed a moderate eating disorder and exercise addiction, so that I didn't sound or look like a bogan. And I wore Ralph Lauren shirts as an alibi. In this way, I was the opposite of ScoMo: I passed as upper-middle-class, and I wanted people to mistake me for a GPS boy.

Dad was a doppelganger of Lech Wałęsa, my namesake, the uneducated electrician who became president of Poland. My knockabout father didn't read the Quarterly Essay. But in reality, he was much more politically engaged than me. Since moving to the home of Bundaberg Rum, that DIY social democrat had joined the local branch of the ALP and become friendly with Queensland Rail employees and United Voice union officials. His flatmate and assistant manager at the motel was a Maori woman fleeing from DV. He employed cleaners through a program for people with a disability. His top three policy obsessions: jobs, jobs and jobs. That night, we sat eating medium-rare rib fillets and baked potatoes for dinner.

"I've got a job for ya," he said at dinner.

Like Kim Beazley in the lead-up to the 2007 election, my father – whose weight was constantly yo-yoing – had dropped twenty kilograms since I last saw him. The reason for this now became clear. The seat of Hinkler needed a candidate for the next election. In 2010, Labor had suffered a 10 per cent swing. The next one would be no better and wasn't attracting a crowded field for preselection. Dad was considering throwing his hat into the ring.

"You could be my campaign manager!" he said, with a grin, but clearly dead serious. "Who cares if we win. Let's stick it to the pricks."

I was flabbergasted, and not just because he was vastly overestimating my professional skillset. Dad was much closer cosmetically and rhetorically to Russell Robertson than Kevin Rudd. To describe his stomach as a beer gut wouldn't be doing it justice. He left school at thirteen to get a job at the abattoir. He did well enough in small business to be classified as middle class by the ATO. Still, old ideologies die hard, and dietary habits even harder.

Dad was an instinctive Keynesian. He appreciated that a larger welfare state meant battlers could afford to buy a counter meal at the pub. He'd been good mates with far more Aboriginal people than the average inner-city member of the ALP. But I knew that cosmopolitans would view him as a bogan, in the same way much of the political establishment in Poland saw Wałęsa. I imagined the middle-class journalists peppering him with gotcha questions. "Aren't you getting a bit long in the tooth for a career change?" I said.

"Youth is wasted on the young," he said. "Bugger ya."

"Labor isn't going to win, anyway," I backtracked. "Why bother?"

"They definitely ain't gonna win with that shit attitude," he said.

Subconsciously, I saw parliament as a place for my classmates at UQ: well-read, PC progressives who could stick to the script. I was mortified by the prospect of him seeking preselection, even if defeat at an election was a foregone conclusion. He didn't look or speak like the media and political class I wanted to belong to. He might blow my cover. On a rational level, I didn't think that the chip on my father's shoulder had an electoral future. I thought that I knew more about economics than a self-made small businessman, more about social equality than a foster carer, more about politics than someone who understood how branch meetings worked.

"What's your honest opinion?" he asked.

"Honestly?" I said. "I think that politics has changed."

"Howzat?"

"The Labor Party will die if it doesn't modernise," I said. "You can't win a federal majority any more just by speaking to the working class."

"Labor will win jack shit without them," he said, before delivering one of his favourite aphorisms about pubs. "You need to give people what they want. Not what *you* want to give them. Or they'll get it from someone else."

Within a few days, my father – who had type 2 diabetes – suffered from kidney failure like his dad. The medication the doctors gave him thinned his blood too much, producing a replica of the stroke that killed his mum. It was five years since a triple heart bypass, and fifteen years since his first major heart attack. His funeral was at Toowoomba's local sporting stadium. Five hundred people travelled from across the state. That weekend, three different country rugby league teams wore black armbands to commemorate Dad's influence. Allan Langer – Queensland rugby league's most beloved larrikin – was a pallbearer. Bruce was both a pallbearer and a eulogist.

"Tommy was an Aussie larrikin," he said, before the speakers played "Imagine" by John Lennon, Dad's favourite song – not "Waltzing Matilda."

Bruce was talking about a different larrikin to Kerry Packer, although they shared superficial similarities, such as a love of sport and gambling. Dad was flawed. But those flaws produced practical compassion. At branch meetings, he argued for the dole and pension to be raised, and the retirement age to be kept at sixty-five, budget deficit be damned. He was pro-soldier and anti-war. In 2010, while president of a state Labor branch, his clique of blue-collar sparkies protested Anna Bligh's plans to privatise public assets. He believed that the greatest act of mateship between the rich and poor was public health care and the redistribution of wealth. Tragically, that kind of Aussie larrikin was endangered.

In hindsight, it was exactly the kind of larrikin the Labor Party should have been embracing to stave off electoral irrelevancy. Not exclusively, and not necessarily as leaders, but prominently enough to make its traditional base feel represented at the highest levels of power. Dropping out of university after my father's death was a godsend, and I never felt much desire to go back. I slowly detoxed from the systematic classism of my private schooling and tertiary education, and stopped feeling so ashamed of my kin, who'd loved me unconditionally despite the throb of my snobbery.

I thought about my father after interviewing Russell Robertson. And I wondered who Labor should be getting to talk to voters like my brother John: university-educated intellectuals, or a coalminer from Clermont named Robbo. Provided that he is equally committed to ambitious climate-change targets, why shouldn't he be a candidate? Coordinating a transition away from coal without coalminers is like trying to design a student curriculum without schoolteachers.

Whenever I miss my father's larrikin intuitions, I pick up the blower to Bruce. He works as a FIFO electrician on a gas mine in the electorate of Flynn, just north of John in Hinkler. Flynn is one of the key seats that Labor wants to win at the 2022 election. Bruce looks and sounds like Paul Hogan, without the botox, hair dye or hatred of tax. His preferred PM is Penny Wong, which goes to show that you shouldn't automatically assume what a top bloke wants.

"Penny Wong's an intelligent bloody woman who's got her heart in the right place," he tells me. "She's got more balls than half the blokes."

Bruce has watched all of his forecasts come true. The new generation of miners, so hostile towards collective action, are getting screwed by mining companies and right-wing politicians, as he predicted twenty years ago when they switched to John Howard and quit the trade unions. The wealth of the tycoons proliferated during the Covid-19 pandemic. Their employees face permanent uncertainty. The coalminer's son reckons that morale is nudging rock-bottom. And the thud might produce a renaissance of working-class solidarity.

"How can you buy a house when property prices keep going berserk," says Bruce, "but workers are still earning the same wage that they were getting five, six years ago? Or they're getting pay cuts. It doesn't bloody add up."

Bruce is two years off retirement, which he plans to spend "playing bowls and drinking piss." He doesn't have dependents. But his carpenter son – who works as a scaffolder on an offshore oilrig in northern Western Australia – has a wife, a child and a mortgage. He is earning the same hourly rate as six years ago. Those who don't suck up the stagnating wages and outright pay cuts – or who complain about unsafe work conditions – are replaced by scabs from labour-hire companies. Bruce believes that the penny is beginning to drop and the lucky country is ripe for a blue-collar revolution.

"The climate *is* changing," says Bruce. "People who don't know that have got their heads in the sand or their fingers in the till. Labor should be out there saying: *they're about to stop buying this fuckin' stuff!* What are my grandkids gonna do for work? These other industries will create a shitload of jobs, mate."

Lachlan Harris says that the only way Labor can win an election on climate change is removing the financial threat felt by coalminers. He is sceptical that the blue-collar parochials of Queensland and the Hunter Valley will be won over by vague promises about "just transitions." Harris believes the Covid-19 budget blowout has given the Opposition the perfect get-out-of-jail-free card for a Keynesian approach to climate change, but that Labor will need to guarantee coalminers a full-time job at the same pay.

"The Left is convinced that it will be good enough to promise people *the green jobs of the future*," he says. "What the fuck does that mean? We've announced lockdowns, without JobKeeper. We could do JobKeeper with every single coalminer … JobKeeper is just the dole with good marketing."

It isn't as crazy as it would have sounded eighteen months ago. Interest rates are historically low, and Covid-19 has shattered the national fetish for surpluses. What's the point of a surplus without a planet? AMWU president Steve Murphy has tried to seize the moment by forming a coalition called the Hunter Jobs Alliance with Felicity Wade, the convener of the Labor Environmental Action Network. Murphy wants Labor to fund publicly owned infrastructure projects linked to renewable energy and regional communities.

"The whole time that we're fighting each other, mining bosses and private capital are winning," says Murphy. "We need to redefine the problems that we all face and build alliances to solve the climate crisis together."

No matter how hypocritical it might seem, Howard and now Morrison have successfully offered the Coalition as the natural home for parochials who want to cast a protest vote against the snobbery of cosmopolitans. The question is what progressives do next. The 2022 election will be a fight between cosmopolitans and parochials. Climate change – Labor's Achilles heel – might actually present the best opportunity to offer vision to cosmopolitans and meat and potatoes to parochials, and to negotiate a ceasefire between environmentalists and miners.

If the larrikin weren't already dead, he would have croaked during Covid-19. Australia removed the mask of anti-authoritarianism to reveal a nation of law-abiding citizens. On Twitter, each lockdown turned into a clash of fake doctors, anti-vaxxers, dobbers and hypochondriacs who love politicians so much they wouldn't tolerate a bad word about them. Annabel Crabb hosted the Australia Talks survey. Nearly 80 per cent of almost 60,000 respondents agreed with the proposition that Australia should keep its borders shut indefinitely until the coronavirus pandemic was over.

"When push comes to shove in this country, the larrikin thing is just not true," says Crabb. "We love a bloody tough border! Whether it's keeping boat people out or keeping Victorians out if they're having [a Covid-19] outbreak. Australians love rules, and we are really good at obeying them."

But it wasn't the widespread acquiescence to border closures and rolling lockdowns that heralded the death of the larrikin, nor the booming popularity of the politicians who brought in the restrictions. It was the airing of a documentary called *The Death of the Aussie Larrikin?* Host Rowan Dean left the question mark hanging, because he was here to rescue anti-authoritarianism, via Sky News. Dean was interviewed about the doco on *The Bolt Report* by Andrew Bolt, a man who makes a six-figure salary from attempting to cancel actual larrikins.

"The scourge of political correctness has tried to put a stranglehold around the Aussie larrikin," said Dean with an Australian flag over one shoulder and an Akubra over the other. "Every Australian now has to choose: am I on the side of the political correctness wowsers? Or am I actually going to stand up for free speech and the genuine larrikin spirit of this nation?"

The silvertails of Australia's right-wing elite weren't even making the effort to wear costumes or feign ocker accents. Bolt wore a blazer with a pocket square. They were giddier than two teenagers after raiding the liquor cabinet at a sleepover. Dean flashed an untouched meat pie and can of VB.

"I've got my beer ready, Andrew," said Dean. "I'm going to watch with the VB. I've got the pie ready … I've got the sauce! I've got the sauce as well!"

"I've got Colonial!" cried Bolt, cackling uncontrollably. "Brilliant!"

The two most thin-skinned wowsers in the Australian media claimed the larrikin tradition as their own, and officially extinguished it. Dean – a Canberra Grammar boy and ex-advertising executive whose "satire" is subsidised by a billionaire – became the official spokesperson of a working-class tradition. Bolt sipped a tinnie like a child receiving 10 millilitres of cough syrup. "Hmmh," said Bolt. "It's actually … very nice!"

I sighed with relief that my publican father wasn't alive to suffer another aneurysm. "'The Aussie Larrikin Is Dead' Says The Last Two Cunts On Earth That You'd Invite To The Pub," reported *The Betoota Advocate*. "In a rare turn of events," wrote editor Clancy Overell, "Sky News has actually produced a television program – as opposed to their usual format of just letting pedophile-apologists say whatever comes into their shiraz-soaked brains on prime-time television without any repercussions."

Melissa Lucashenko still sees evidence of the larrikin tradition, but in the ratbags on the fringes of society, usually within racial minorities, the underclass, the incarcerated and the mentally ill. She points at the example of Tracker Tilmouth mooning a racist redneck at a polling booth as a classic act of larrikinism. But she says that Tracker had the protection of a public profile. "Doomadgee sings 'Who Let the Dogs Out' to the coppers and ends up dead," she says. "The larrikin is a stereotype that situates white lawlessness as harmless and fun and desirable if it's a white dude. Whereas the same behaviour could get a black man thrown in jail or possibly killed."

After the Black Lives Matter protests – incessantly condemned by Sky News – Lucashenko witnessed a Pacific Islander woman getting arrested at a shopping centre in suburban Brisbane. There were two cop cars and five coppers. Lucashenko recorded the arrest on her phone. She tells me this discreet act of anti-authoritarianism elicited outrage and abuse from passers-by, including a woman who told her that they weren't in America. "I fail to see Australians having any serious commitment to anti-authoritarianism, or the underdog, or the swagman," says Lucashenko. "Most of them would suck a copper's dick quicker than you can spit."

Lidia Thorpe is fighting for a treaty and more direct Aboriginal representation in parliament. The daughter of a single mum, she grew up in council housing and admits to getting into punch-ups all the time at school. Thorpe empathises with the battlers. She wants to talk about climate change and economics in a way people living in the towers can understand. And she's happy to use the c-word. "Absolutely there's class in Australia," she tells me. "You see photos of people sitting outside flash cafés sipping their lattes while blackfellas sleep in doorways beside the café … The truth is coming out. People are seeing – particularly through Covid – the inequality that exists in this country."

There is more larrikin spirit in the fingernail of Thorpe's left pinkie than in Rowan Dean and Andrew Bolt put together. But she definitely doesn't want to be called a "larrikin." She sees the tradition as too "white-washed" and too "man-washed." And she isn't following the ghosts of Lawson and Hawke. "I'm very optimistic," she says. "I think I'm here for a reason. My ancestors will guide me. I'm the vehicle. But we're running out of time. Climate change isn't just at our doorstep. It's flowing through the doors."

Omar Sakr refuses to fit the politically correct, social-justice-warrior stereotype railed against by Bolt and Dean. Sakr takes issue with the right and the left. After high school, Sakr enrolled in creative writing at the University of Technology. It was far from the bastion of open-minded enlightenment imagined by the people who attend such institutions.

"First year of uni, people had a look of blank incomprehension on their faces when I told them that I went to Liverpool Boys High," he tells me. "Students whose parents paid tens of thousands of dollars a year for them to go to high school, whose parents would buy them places … In that moment, you become aware of how wide the gap is. It's really alienating."

Class is the elephant in the corner of both the arts and the progressive left. The bisexual Arab-Australian poet – "I'm very aware of the rarity of my existence," he laughs – found Bulldogs games at Belmore Oval a nirvana compared to creative writing workshops. Sakr says the diversity of the western suburbs – a place often stigmatised as a wasteland of poor migrants and white bogans – produced creative stimulation and authentic acts of tolerance.

"I would honestly come across more progressive opinions from the tradie down the street than I would in so-called leftie arts spaces," says Sakr. "A lot of the people who think that they're progressive and egalitarian have the same managerial mindset as conservatives … And woe fucking betide you if you give them any shit. You're their evidence of being a good person."

Sakr tells me that he doesn't believe in solidarity. He is sceptical of collectivism, and he certainly doesn't worship at the altar of the larrikin, or any of Australia's other myths of egalitarianism. I started writing this essay as a way to reclaim the working-class larrikin from the cosplay coalminers of the Coalition and the billionaire squatters camouflaged as down-to-earth swagmen. But at this point, it seems pretty delusional for me to expect the victims of larrikinism to rehabilitate the myths used to dispossess Aboriginal people, mistreat women and imprison asylum seekers.

"If Ned Kelly's name was Abdul," says Sakr, "I'm telling you right now, that's not a national myth this country would be in love with."

Abdul Abdullah has been shortlisted for the Archibald Prize five times, first for a portrait of Waleed Aly. He has painted Anthony Mundine and Craig Campbell, the copper who flogged ringleaders of the Cronulla Riots with a baton, before being ostracised by the NSW Police Force. In 2019, Abdullah's paintings were displayed in the Sarina Art Gallery, and came to the attention of Nationals MP George Christensen. Christensen took exception to Abdullah's portrait of a melancholy Australian soldier overlaid with a smiley emoji. The decorated artist was critiquing the public expectation that traumatised war veterans fit the bill of the happy-go-lucky larrikin. Christensen – a whip-cracking maverick whose career is built around a fetish for free speech – tried to cancel Abdullah's free speech.

"The Australian and Queensland Governments – yes, my own bloody Government – have funded this 'art' which so openly attacks our troops," he wrote in a Facebook post. Christensen famously charged taxpayers $3000 for connecting flights to visit Manila, where he spent three hundred days over a four-year period, missing parliamentary hearings in the process.

The painting caused a furore. Abdullah received racist hate mail. His artworks were removed from the Sarina gallery. Abdullah's father – whose convict forebear arrived in Australia on *The Indefatigable* – noticed the bitter irony of his son getting attacked by a FIFO career politician. "Christensen," said Ibrahim Abdullah. "What's that name? Scandinavian?"

Abdullah's paternal grandfather was a World War II veteran. Both of his great-grandfathers were World War I veterans. His Malaysian grandfather served in the British Navy during World War II. Abdullah has a tattoo of the Southern Cross on his ribs, with the crescent moon of Islam in the middle. But Sakr was right: a bloke named Abdul isn't allowed to be a larrikin. Abdul Abdullah was thinking about George Christensen – and the gang of right-wing larrikins that he belongs to – while working on a landscape painting entitled "The Waltz." In white block letters over the kind of rolling hills beloved by bush poets, Abdullah pinpointed Australia's identity crisis.

THEY THINK THEY'RE THE SWAGMAN
BUT THEY'RE ALL SQUATTERS AND COPS

"I don't think the larrikin is dead," says Abdullah. "I just think it's been co-opted by the toffs and their middle managers. It's cultural appropriation of the working-class by the elite, made ugly by the swaggering confidence of power and wealth."

Perhaps there is no point fighting Rowan Dean for the copyright of an expression already so hollowed out. Let him have "The Larrikin," at least the capital-l version that demands conformity to a majoritarian ideal of national identity imposed by white-collar propagandists. Small-l larrikins will continue to exist on the fringes of society, with or without the approval of Andrew Bolt. Who cares what we call them?

"Once you've exploded the myth that the Australian larrikin needs to be a virile, white, heterosexual man, you allow all others sorts of anti-authoritarian figures to be embraced by Australian culture," says Clare Wright.

Joel Thompson is a picture of virility. The Indigenous All Stars captain and Manly Sea Eagles second rower is 190 centimetres tall and weighs 105 kilograms. I drive four hours southwest from Sydney to meet Thompson in the flesh. He has a tattoo of an Aboriginal flag on his neck. Thompson is doing a mental health workshop at the Gundagai RSL. "G'day, Slug," says Thompson to a mulleted man wearing a polo shirt for the Gundagai Tigers, the local rugby league team which won the premiership a month earlier. Slug's collarbone is in a sling. "Have a good year?" asks Thompson. "The Tigers? Mate, how good!" If the script sounds familiar, it's because Morrison imitates the lingo of blokes like Joel Thompson. "Cya, boys," he says at the end. "Cya, Slug."

I stay at the Poets Recall Motel. It has plaques dedicated to a bush poet outside each room. The next morning, I catch up with Thompson in the park across the road from the RSL. Unlike Henry Lawson, Thompson doesn't need a sketch artist to give him thicker wrists. Most of the tattoos have been removed from Thompson's ripped forearms. But a poem dedicated to his Aboriginal nan remains visible. He also has the landscape of Ivanhoe – the place that feels most like home – tattooed across his back. In Ivanhoe, population 200, Thompson's teenage mum fell pregnant to the son of a white farmer. "I felt like I was stuck in two different worlds," Thompson tells me. "Who am I? People would tell me that I was too white to be black. Or that I was too black to be white."

Joel Thompson was born in Griffith, grew up in Ivanhoe and lived with step-parents in Gundagai and Wagga Wagga. His struggling mum turned to the drug trade. He spent much of his childhood travelling between domestic violence shelters and stealing food from the lunchboxes of white classmates. Thompson's nan fostered him at thirteen. He believes that she saved him from jail. For the first time, he went to school with a packed lunchbox. But he still broke into houses and stole cars out of habit. Thompson's biological dad found him a rugby league scholarship at a Catholic boarding school in Forbes. "Boarding school was like arriving on a different planet," he tells me. "The other kids hadn't seen the things I'd seen. I didn't even know how to use a knife and fork. Or how to have a disagreement without violence."

Thompson debuted as an NRL player at the age of nineteen. Having grown up in a housing commission area, he knew nobody who owned their own home. He confesses to wasting most of his nouveau riches on "pokies, grog, drugs." A high-profile professional athlete, Thompson used alcohol to self-medicate his flashbacks to childhood trauma and suicidal impulses.

"I had to be the larrikin," he says. "I had to be fun Joel. It was like I was an actor. I'd always have to go into different characters. I'd go home and take the mask off and suffer by myself … My wife saved my life. She goes: 'We're gonna get you some help.' I got diagnosed with type II bipolar. It runs in my family."

Joel Thompson has played 252 professional games of possibly the toughest contact sport in the world. He spent his final season in the NRL with the Manly Sea Eagles, the team nicknamed "the Silvertails" by Roy Masters. Thompson – an itinerant fibro from western New South Wales – now lives on the northern beaches. But he doesn't feel any nostalgia for the existential battles of the underclass. "I've jumped classes," he says. "Sydney's a different world. My kids are going to school with little rich white kids. But I know how tough it is on the other side. There's no point glorifying it. I've got two little brothers in and out of juvi. I was lucky that I had rugby league. My brothers didn't have that lottery ticket."

Thompson's biggest battle is with bipolar. He has become a prominent mental health advocate. The project is ongoing. In 2019, during a manic episode, he went off his medication and got blackout drunk. He fell down a steep hill and smashed his head so hard on a rock that he could have died of blood loss. When we meet, Thompson hasn't touched a drop of grog in twelve months, except for a glass of red wine with his wife at the end of the NRL season. He is doing workshops in Gundagai, Wagga Wagga, Griffiths, Ivanhoe and Goolgowi. The cause is personal and urgent: a few months ago, his cousin in Ivanhoe took her life. Thompson has also lost male cousins to suicide.

"My project is all about unmasking the larrikin," says Thompson. "And changing the narrative about what a man needs to be. You don't need to keep everything bottled up. That whole macho mentality nearly killed me."

Thompson didn't watch the first game of the 2020 State of Origin series. The NRL had recently decided not to play the national anthem before State of Origin matches, out of respect to the Indigenous players who refuse to sing it. This should have been uncontroversial: the game was between Queensland and New South Wales, not Australia and New Zealand. But Scott Morrison reportedly pressured the NRL into backflipping. Heavily reliant on the government to play games during the Covid-19 pandemic, it caved. The prime minister remained preoccupied with fighting superficial Culture Wars, even during a global pandemic. He had time to call the chairman of the NRL about the national anthem, but not the global CEO of Pfizer about securing vaccinations. The Indigenous All Stars captain was furious.

"The PM came in and said: Nah, youse need to sing this song," he says. "We're not a big enough number to swing votes … [ScoMo] is just a character he plays, mate. You'd love some of these people making decisions to be out in Aboriginal communities. We face challenges most of them have never witnessed."

Thompson escaped poverty through professional rugby league and found self-acceptance through the Indigenous All Stars. He has been an outspoken supporter of Latrell Mitchell, the star fullback for the South Sydney Rabbitohs. Mitchell – a proud Aboriginal man – refused to sing the national anthem before a 2019 State of Origin game. He is frequently vilified by the media and racially abused by fans on social media. Joel Thompson is sick of the trolls, and pissed at Morrison for tacitly legitimising their persecution. But he is optimistic that his daughters will inherit a more tolerant society, thanks to trailblazers such as Adam Goodes.

"We're in a big war," says Thompson. "My grandmother was punished and demonised. She stayed silent. But Adam Goodes stood up against all the boos, against the majority of Australia, against the Establishment. I was at the march on Australia Day. More people are having voices. More people are coming together."

The larrikin is dead. Long live the larrikin! Anti-authoritarianism doesn't need the vocabulary of the bush poets, the accent of Mick Dundee or the imprimatur of the shock jocks and media tycoons to inspire social change. It sounds like Grace Tame, and acts like Behrouz Boochani, and looks like Adam Goodes.

In May 2019, Anthony Albanese was elected unopposed as leader of the federal ALP by a caucus still deeply rocked by the shock election loss. This was a victory for true believers in the gospel of the fair go. A top bloke who was raised in council housing by a single mum on a disability pension had become leader of the federal Opposition. His obsession with rugby league was a substantial part of the leadership pitch. Despite representing a cosmopolitan electorate, Albanese was seen as the ALP's best option to reach beyond inner-city Sydney and Melbourne to outer-suburban Brisbane and regional Queensland. He could offer Australia a dinky-di larrikin.

"To me, the larrikin is a part of our egalitarian spirit," Albanese tells me. "We don't bow before authority in this country."

Anthony Albanese was hypothetically right up my alley. As a teenager, I lived in an unfashionable suburb with a single mum on a disability pension, although she owned her own home. More importantly, Albanese was a die-hard South Sydney Rabbitohs fan, a team that I took a liking to as a small kid thanks to an Aboriginal halfback named Darrell "Tricky" Trindall, whom I considered the black Allan Langer. As a seven-year-old, I was devastated when the club was kicked out of the NRL. Albanese was one of the key figures who led the street marches saving the club from the brink of extinction.

But Albanese becoming Labor leader also elicited disappointment from those who aren't male, white or diehard rugby league fans. At a time of unprecedented diversity in parliament and Australian society, the style of leadership available to a potential prime minister seemed to be growing narrower. Both of the major parties were led by self-proclaimed underdogs from suburban Sydney pushing a wheelbarrow for the Aussie battler. Neither Morrison nor Albanese would describe themselves as full-blown larrikins, but their public personas are thoroughly constructed around that myth: the love of rugby league and a beer, the lack of airs and graces. Pretentiousness offends them. They aren't too opinionated, mate, and they prefer concrete policy solutions to intellectual abstractions.

The fact that Morrison's authenticity is a performance doesn't actually matter that much to his supporters. I present the overwhelming evidence to my brother John that ScoMo is a Pentecostal rah-rah from the eastern suburbs, not one of us. "Maybe you're right," says John. "But who gives a shit? He's a politician, not a priest." The point isn't that Morrison – or Donald Trump – are actual battlers, but how they make outsiders like John feel. The parochials want to see someone who respects them in power, because they rarely feel seen or heard by the cosmopolitans.

Lachlan Harris accuses the major parties of tapping into the larrikin myth, rather than trying to innovate a fresh vernacular for the Australian dream and reach beyond their traditional bases. Harris has been "in the belly of the beast" and confesses that apparatchiks like him imagine swinging voters in marginal seats resemble characters from *Wake in Fright*, rather than being complex people with a capacity to understand big ideas. "The idea that the country is filled with simplistic, self-interested voters who just want a bloke who goes to the footy and eats Four'n Twenty Pies is fucking bullshit," he says. "But political parties are truth creation machines."

Harris says describing Albanese's policy agenda as "small target" is clever advertising for the absence of audacity. He admits helping Rudd beat Howard with a small target. But he insists 2022 won't be déjà vu. For one thing, he says, Albanese doesn't have Rudd's inexplicable cult of personality. For another, voters are much more sensitive to political risk than in the boom times of 2007. After they shuffle reluctantly into the booth at their local school or church, Harris is convinced swinging voters will go with the top bloke they know, unless Labor offers them something with a bit more flavour.

"Albo and ScoMo are the Pizza Hut and Domino's of Australian politics," he says. "They are a throwback to a time when everyone was forced to eat the same food, listen to the same music, watch the same TV shows. But change is coming at a million miles an hour. You can smell it in Canberra. Everyone's shitting themselves, because none of them know what to do."

*

If Anthony Albanese is crapping his daks, he's keeping a straight face. It is May 2021. "G'day, mate," says Australia's Opposition leader. "I'm Albo." Albanese drops an f-bomb about a box left on his desk. We sit on the twenty-first floor of 1 Bligh Street, named after the governor who was cut down by the Rum Rebellion. I'm a long way from Bundaberg. Through lustrous shutters, the Harbour Bridge fuses two sides of the same inner-city elite. A framed poster of Bob Hawke grins at us from the wall behind Albo's desk.

"People say to me that the Labor Party isn't what it used to be," he says. "And I say: no, we now have women in the parliament … We now don't support the White Australia policy, which was one of the four planks that Labor Party had as its core at Federation. We are now concerned about First Nations people. We now support equality on the basis of people's sexuality."

The Opposition leader is wearing blue suede shoes, black socks, grey chinos and a white button-up with no tie. The black socks are colour-matched with the belt, and the blue shoes colour-matched with the blazer. Albanese has lost thirteen kilograms by giving up drinking and swimming twice a week. This adds to the gradual cosmetic improvements since realising that he was a leadership candidate, circa 2013. Albo 2.0 doesn't conjure up someone who smashes schooners of beer or fights Tories. He looks like the after photo of a *Queer Eye for the Straight Guy* makeover. "One of the things that Tom [Uren] said to me once is that you can be more radical in a conservative suit," he tells me.

This is the opposite of Kerry Packer wearing a tracksuit to Redfern Oval. Albanese is a fibro in the sheep's clothing of a silvertail. He has undergone an asymmetrical reinvention to Morrison's. Shadow frontbenchers such as Terri Butler conspicuously refer to him as Anthony, not Albo. Albanese *wants* to be seen as a serious politician, not a class war–fighting larrikin eyeing the franking credits of retirees and the inheritances of their grandkids.

In the abstract, Australians love a larrikin. But they don't want to be led by a full-blown loose cannon, or they would have sided with Mark Latham – the unhinged maverick from western Sydney – over John Howard, the safe-as-houses wowser. They elected Hawke precisely because his larrikinism might tame the trade unions. He seemed a safer option than Fraser. ScoMo was just ocker enough to make voters feel like they were in familiar hands. But fundamentally, he wanted the country to stay the same.

This is the uncomfortable reality Albanese has confronted head-on: there is no vast reservoir of untapped left-wing sentiment in the suburbs. Australians are much less egalitarian-minded than they keep telling pollsters. At the crunch, the majority will opt for the leader who poses the least perceived risk to their personal finances. Labor's new plan is to give those debt-addled aspirationals what they want, not what social democrats want to give them.

"I've been around a long time," says Linda Burney, who attributes her place in parliament to the mentorship and factional lobbying of Albanese. "I think I know what it takes to fight Tories. It requires pragmatism."

Not long after I interview Albanese, Labor officially abandons changes to franking credits and negative gearing, and drops its opposition to stage three of the Coalition's tax cuts. By 2024, everyone earning between $40,000 and $200,000 will pay the same tax rate of 30 per cent. It will cost the budget approximately $19 billion a year. The basic principle of progressive taxation might not survive Covid-19. This provokes profound disillusionment in someone writing an essay about Australia's cult of inequality. But the ALP hardheads have decided that an election can't be won while diverging from the Liberals on tax policy. And they're probably right. Rudd and Swan made the same judgment before the 2007 election, when they matched Howard's middle-class welfare. In 2019, even modest deviations opened the floodgates for a scare campaign about death duties.

Terri Butler refuses to apologise for ideological impurity. She estimates that 97 per cent of the people complaining about Labor dropping cancer and dental policies weren't aware that they existed at the 2019 election. "Would I prefer that the people of Australia had an appetite for negative-gearing reform that we could tap into to win an election?" she asks rhetorically. "Yes! But if they don't, we shouldn't just sit around designing policies for the way the world should be, rather than the way the world is."

To the frustration of progressives, Albanese has followed Labor's 2019 election review to the nth degree. He wants to have a conversation with socially conservative parochials in the suburbs and regions, not chase after the small-l Liberals who speculate about voting Labor if they find a leader with "charisma." Whether or not Albanese wins the next election, this basic understanding of arithmetic will be the defining theme of his leadership.

"We got 48 per cent of the vote last time around," he tells me. "We're 2 per cent short. We need to not just talk to the 48 per cent who voted for us."

Albanese doesn't radiate a sense of superiority, either on TV or in the flesh. I feel no insecurity while interviewing him, or a comedic undertow to his rhetoric. Even Rudd had contradictions between his public and private self – the Queensland farm boy turned Mandarin-speaking intellectual – that gave everything he said a slightly ironic quality. There have been some renovations, and attempts to communicate more clearly, but Albo is undeniably Anthony Albanese, whether you like him or loathe him.

"The NSW Left always loses," says Butler. "So to be a senior person in that world for such a long time requires having strong enough convictions that you are willing to cop a whole lot of shit, while losing a lot … Well before it was Labor Party orthodoxy, Anthony was at our conferences plugging away at marriage equality. He's got values that he's had for his whole life."

Losing so much has made Albo extremely risk-averse. He doesn't think the universe owes him the prime ministership. This missing sense of destiny is extremely disconcerting to progressives who are nostalgic for someone to worship, and conservatives who are nostalgic for someone to revile. In other words, Albanese gives political aficionados the shits. The only people I interviewed who predicted Anthony Albanese winning the next election with any confidence were Anthony Albanese, Kevin Rudd and loyal members of Labor's shadow cabinet. Most of the progressive naysayers suggested a change to Tanya Plibersek. A Coalition MP implored Labor with a curious passion that they needed to switch to Richard Marles, a Geelong Grammar old boy who looks and sounds the part.

The bipartisan consensus has been that Albo is a nice bloke, but not prime minister material. At times, I've shared some of the doubts, mostly owing to Australia's indomitable media monopoly and the benefit of incumbency following a pandemic. But I also think there is a much stronger probability Labor would lose the next election with a leader who members of the media and political class find "charismatic" – that old chestnut – rather than one who's a little bit dull for their liking. Indeed, slow and steady will be just what the doctor ordered.

"If you do nothing but watch politics, of course you'd prefer to have somebody who is sparkling and witty," says Annabel Crabb, who admits to membership of the media class. "All [swinging voters] want is a leader who doesn't give them a heart attack every five minutes. Predictability, stability."

Almost all of the people who said Albanese couldn't win compared him to Whitlam, Hawke or Keating, and not to the last Labor leader to achieve a federal majority: Kevin Rudd. Albo 2.0 is Kevin07 without the church visits and big words, basically. In 1972, Whitlam was trying to convert middle-class Liberal voters in suburban Sydney and Melbourne, especially women. In 1983, Hawke faced much the same electoral equation. They already had most of the working class sewn up.

Thanks to Labor's influx of university-educated cosmopolitans and the departure of Howard's Battlers, the group of people who decide elections in 2022 is extremely different to 1972. Albanese's path to victory includes winning back parochials in regional Queensland and Tasmania, especially blue-collar men, many of whom voted for One Nation in 2019. Terri Butler believes that pundits too often ignore the example of a female Labor leader with a proven track record of attracting Howard's Battlers. "If you want to see the kind of leader who can win seats in Queensland," she says, "have a look at Annastacia Palaszczuk."

In Queensland, Labor has governed for twenty of the last twenty-three years, while consistently shunning the ALP at a federal level. There was evidently more to Peter Beattie's success than being a top bloke. Annastacia Palaszczuk has inherited his pragmatic approach to politics. She doesn't have a charismatic bone in her body. Yet a twice-divorced woman without children has become the first female political leader in Australia to be re-elected twice, and in the state commonly regarded as the most conservative.

Albanese won't have Palaszczuk's benefit of incumbency. But if the federal One Nation vote evaporates, Labor could win seats such as Flynn and Capricornia, despite the artificially high margins. Needless to say, Pauline Hanson sympathisers aren't longing for the vision of Whitlam, the charisma of Hawke or the wit of Keating. Charm isn't an attractive quality to voters who fundamentally distrust politicians. It comes across as smugness.

"Albo?" says my brother John. "I don't have a strong opinion on him. Seems like a nerdier sort of guy. But down-to-earth. A bit like John Howard."

At a visceral level, Albanese would bristle at the juxtaposition. Albo 1.0 hated Howard so much he reportedly used his clout at the Rabbitohs to veto him becoming the boss of rugby league. At a strategic level, the comparison would be music to the ears of ALP hardheads. Howard is the model of leadership not just for winning the next election but for changing the country from humble beginnings. Shortly before the 1996 election, *Four Corners* broadcast "An Average Australian Bloke." Democrats founder Don Chipp accused John Howard of "being a man almost totally without charisma" and capitulating to Labor on the republic, private health care and industrial relations. Host Liz Jackson grilled Howard about not believing in anything and swinging with the wind.

"Fourteen per cent see Keating as indecisive," she said. "Thirty-two per cent see you as indecisive."

"And about 150 per cent of all of the people polled don't trust him," said Howard, laughing good-naturedly. "So I think he's got a problem."

With the benefit of hindsight, nobody would accuse John Howard of not believing in anything, or of being too indecisive on the monarchy, private health care and industrial relations. But he realised that the best vehicle for his beliefs was achieving a majority. It wasn't easy. He needed to train the Liberals to prefer winning to the feeling of moral superiority, and not to declare every single policy ambition *before* getting elected, like John Hewson did in 1993.

The other key similarity between Albanese and Howard is experience. Albanese has suffered the adrenaline rush of victory and promotion to the senior ranks of government, followed by the depression of defeat. He appreciates the difficulty of winning and the art of governing. Expecting Albanese to become the left-wing equivalent of Howard would be optimistic. But he is consistently criticised for not showing the sort of policy backbone that Hawke and Howard didn't grow until after victory.

"I think the Left sometimes has a romanticism about the past," says Albanese. "I was there in 1983. Hawkey's campaign was 'Bringing Australia Together.' And we'll have a summit afterwards and decide what to do."

Those hoping for the street-marching larrikin of old to reappear at the last minute will be sorely disappointed. Albanese is offering a grocery list of policies on childcare, wage growth, industrial relations and public infrastructure projects, especially social housing. Climate change will be framed as an opportunity for job creation in regional Australia.

"We need to win in the outer suburbs of the capital cities," says Terri Butler. "And we need to win in regional Queensland and Tasmania. That's the ball game. Anthony's the man to do it. He is focusing on the issues that actually matter to the people in the seats that decide elections."

*

Scott Morrison is finding it extremely hard to lay a glove on the top bloke whose identity he stole, and not just because Labor's policy fruit bowl is so empty at the moment. Malcolm Turnbull – or Julie Bishop – might have attacked Albo for being a throwback, and linked the absence of ideological friction to a lack of imagination. It might not have worked, but there would be a clear contrast. For ScoMo to take the same tack would require committing identity suicide. The broader problem for Morrison is that his persona was created for the swallow of a campaign, not the long, hot summer of bushfires and coronavirus.

"It said a lot that when Scott Morrison was quarantining in the Lodge after he went overseas [it] wasn't [with] his economic adviser, wasn't

[with] his foreign affairs adviser, wasn't [with] his national security adviser," Albanese tells me. "It was his photographer. That was the priority. Things like putting together the chicken coop with a drill, even though it needs an Allen key. The red carpet off the plane. The *Top Gun* soundtrack … It's more ProMo than ScoMo."

The prime minister wears the mask of a larrikin without the people skills or street smarts that come from battle scars. The real Scott John Morrison was there for all to see when the PM smoke-bombed to Hawaii during a national disaster, and when he proclaimed: "I don't hold a hose, mate." Voters watched him attempting to put the mask back on while forcing a bushfire victim to shake his hand in Cobargo. They saw the mask fall off completely when he vacillated on the alleged rape of Brittany Higgins, or while claiming he didn't appreciate the seriousness of the situation before a bedside confessional with Jenny.

"I think there is zero possibility that he didn't know," says Albanese. "He mightn't have known all the details. But he must've known there'd been an incident in the defence minister's office prior to that election, because he would've been briefed on it."

The gap between the gravity of those situations and the PM's emotions is the symptom of someone constantly trying to decide whether he needs to be Scott John Morrison or ScoMo. Paul Hogan wasn't expected to wrestle with actual crocodiles, as the prime minister is with the Australian public and the press gallery. Cynicism about Morrison's relationship with the truth has spread from the Canberra Bubble to Quiet Australians in the suburbs and country towns. The suspicion weakening his support with women is that he doesn't care. The suspicion that will weaken him with men is that he has "no ticker."

"It wasn't surprising to me that no one senior went out to the [March for Justice] rally," says Albanese. "If he had of gone out there, people would've respected that. Like they respected Howard for fronting the gun rallies."

The straw that will break the camel's back among voters of both genders is the creeping realisation that Morrison is incompetent and shirks responsibility. It was one thing for him to go missing during the bushfires, or to be mates with Tim Stewart and Brian Houston. But the bungled vaccine rollout and mixed messages on lockdowns are hitting a critical mass of people in the hip pocket – and consistently pissing them off – in a way the other missteps and contradictions didn't. Judging by my Facebook feed, Quiet Australians in regional Queensland have started drawing the same conclusion as tourism executives across two countries.

Kevin Rudd believes that even disengaged voters are developing a sense that something is "not quite right" about the Morrison government. He predicts that Albanese can win the next election by incessantly hammering the Coalition on the public corruption of sports rorts and car parks, and by focusing on bread-and-butter policy issues, such as Robodebt, the NDIS and Medicare. Rudd wants Labor to keep its policies simple. He tells me that Albanese's authenticity will articulate his values, and that Labor needs to painstakingly deconstruct Scott Morrison's daggy dad persona.

"Morrison seeks to be the 'Everyman' of Australian politics," Rudd wrote in 2018. "But beneath the cultivated veneer of suburban mediocrity lies a hard, right-wing Pentecostal and ideological Christian."

One of the accusations frequently levelled against Scott Morrison is that he doesn't believe in anything. But make no mistake: Morrison knows exactly what he believes, and what he achieves by compromising on certain beliefs to keep the Liberal Party in power. Coronavirus has been a golden opportunity to redistribute wealth to the rich. Alan Kohler at *The New Daily* has estimated $30 billion was paid unnecessarily to profitable companies through JobKeeper. Andrew Leigh estimates that the wealth of Australian billionaires doubled in 2020. Meanwhile, the government has continued to cut university funding and make it more expensive for students to study the humanities. Leigh quotes Warren Buffet: "There's class warfare, all right, but it's my class, the rich class, that's making war, and we're winning."

"It's really striking to see a university-educated cabinet – many of whom have liberal arts degrees – increasing university fees during a pandemic," Leigh tells me. "Morrison is fighting a deliberate Culture War against universities. Howard did it a bit. But Morrison's done it much more."

Labor's defrocking of Morrison is a delicate balancing act. By going too hard, Albanese might seem small-minded during a national emergency, or evoke the pettiness of Mark Latham. And by making the attacks on the façade of "suburban mediocrity" too personal – or critiquing the evangelism underneath it – Labor risks insulting the very people it is trying to win over, such as blue-collar tradies and rugby league fans in the regions, and Christians in the outer suburbs of the capital cities.

"The daggy dad persona is obviously all bullshit," says Terri Butler. "That's why Morrison hates parliament: his real personality comes out. He's actually an angry, angry man. And he can't mask that in Question Time. So it's always a good opportunity for us to hold his feet to the fire."

On the PM's Pentecostalism, current Labor MPs walk on eggshells, even off-the-record, afraid to antagonise religious voters they've been shedding since Rudd. Morrison's colleagues are less civil. Coalition MPs from traditional denominations or with secular sympathies view his religion with suspicion and outright derision. Their reservations have been quelled for the sake of unity, but they might be about to stop biting their tongues. On 5 August 2021, Brian Houston was charged with concealing paedophilia. In July 2019, Scott Morrison prayed on stage with Houston at the Hillsong Conference, while aware of the allegations against him. In September 2019, Morrison attempted to score his spiritual mentor an invitation to a dinner at the White House. Donald Trump's administration rejected the request. Morrison repeatedly denied making the invitation, calling it fake news, before confessing to it on talkback radio in January 2020.

"I've known Brian for a long time," he said.

To say that there are a number of Coalition MPs – federal and state – watching the developments with popcorn is an understatement. Those I spoke to who know the PM personally were more damning of the man than Labor MPs. They paint a picture of a prime minister who is publicly supple and privately stubborn. Much bad blood bubbles around NSW factional Svengali Alex Hawke, and most hotly towards former housemate Stuart Robert, who both have strong personal connections to Hillsong.

"With Morrison and his acolytes, it's not so much the overt Christianity," says a senior colleague. "It's more the *we're better than everyone else* attitude."

On a Friday night at the height of lockdown, as anti-ScoMo memes proliferate across social media, Albo uploads his pitch for the prime ministership to Instagram: a picture of a medium-rare steak with two big dollops of canned corn and green peas. The aesthetic is more single dad than daggy dad. But Albanese wants to be seen as a meat-and-two-veg kind of guy. Labor is banking that Australia will grow sick of the mad stepdads running the country and put the technocrats back in charge.

"We need to kick with the wind in the last quarter," he tells me.

The latest Newspoll is released on Sunday night. For the second time in a row, it has Labor ahead 53–47 on the two-party-preferred vote. The prime minister's personal ratings plunge into negative territory for the first time since he disappeared to Hawaii. The next day, the Intergovernmental Panel on Climate Change releases its first major update in eight years, showing that the world will warm 1.5 degrees by 2040 without the urgent slashing of emissions. The UN secretary-general calls the report "a code red for humanity," a well-timed reminder to a sleep-deprived essayist on a final deadline that this isn't *all* a simulation.

"We're on a burning platform," says Terri Butler. "The bad guys are in charge. And they're climate-change deniers! I think that kicking the bad guys out of the Lodge is more important than winning arguments on Twitter."

A few months ago, Morrison claimed that vaccinations weren't a race. Now the everyman-in-chief wants his compatriots to listen to the doctors – not the shock jocks – just this once. ScoMo looks like he's seen a ghost, or at least the feedback from a focus group. Australians are crying out for a sober statesman, not a beer-breathed bloke bellowing "Go Sharks!" With half the country in lockdown, the prime minister tries to bring the bickering factions together with an Olympic-themed metaphor. "It doesn't matter how you start the race," says Morrison. "It is how you finish the race … We are going to finish this race and we are going to race all the way to the finish line. But we are going to do it as Team Australia."

The problem is that the Coalition — and their media and mining allies — have spent the past twenty-five years dividing Team Australia into rival tribes. Howard built an electoral coalition from the Culture War between battlers and elites. Abbott destroyed two Labor prime ministers by waging a Climate War against objectivity. In April, Morrison didn't see a place on Team Australia for the millions of people who eat dinner and drink wine in the metropolitan areas where he has spent his entire life.

"We will not achieve net zero in the cafes, dinner parties and wine bars of our inner cities," he declared at a Business Council of Australia dinner in Martin Place, the heart of the inner city. "It will be won in places like the Pilbara, the Hunter, Gladstone, Portland, Whyalla, Bell Bay and the Riverina. In the factories of our regional towns and outer suburbs."

Barnaby Joyce spent his stint in the sin bin publicly railing against the government, while privately begging MPs for a promotion. Joyce moved within striking distance in June 2021. Acting deputy PM Michael McCormack made a last-ditch pitch to the National Party by calling for the mass relocation of wild mice into the inner-city apartments of animal rights activists. Question Time had descended into larrikin karaoke, and Joyce was always going to win. The Beetrooter returned as Nationals leader on 21 June. He criticised the pursuit of zero Covid cases and begged for the condemnation of Victorians.

"In country areas we couldn't really give a shit," said Joyce, shortly before being fined $200 for not wearing a mask indoors. "We've got record exports of coal. Record exports of beef. But we look at Melbourne, and go, you can almost smell the burning flesh from here."

Australia — a nation of self-proclaimed straight-shooters — has been hijacked by a pack of fabricated larrikins and bona fide bullshit artists. For a quarter-century, Australia's conservative establishment has profited from pitting working-class battlers against the inner-city elite, top blokes against tall poppies, coalmines against universities, larrikins against feminists and gays, patriots against Aboriginals, Muslims and asylum seekers. Public trust in government was systematically sullied by some of the most powerful people in the country. This was a genius strategic move when the enemy was progressive taxation, affordable housing and a price on carbon. But Covid-19 shows no respect for the battlelines of the Culture and Climate Wars.

Now the chickens might finally be coming home to roost for the Liberals, who are trying to unify the country they conquered by dividing. As Alan Jones rails against coronavirus restrictions and the op-ed pages fill with conspiracies, the front page of News Corp and Nine papers are adorned with ads from Clive Palmer. "Lockdowns destroy jobs," they say. "We can never trust the Liberal or Labor parties again!"

Labor isn't the only major party with a fragile electoral marriage, or that is susceptible to the fake news of shock jocks and mining tycoons. Morrison is wedged between Australia's loud majority of wowsers who want lockdowns and mass vaccinations, and libertarian larrikins protesting on the streets and within the National Party, such as George Christensen. "We swear by the Southern Cross to stand truly by each other and fight to defend our rights and liberties," said Christensen in parliament, quoting Peter Lalor. "That is the diggers' oath; the oath taken by Australians in the gold-mining town of Ballarat before they took a fateful stand against tyranny in what we now know as the Eureka Stockade ... We the people want our freedom back. We demand that there be no more lockdowns. We demand that there be no more curfews. We demand that there be no more mask mandates."

Anthony Albanese calls the Coalition "an Opposition in exile on the government benches." Will Howard Battlers be tempted to bury the hatchet with Labor for the sake of a cabinet that actually wants the job of crafting public policy and governing the country? My brother John has voted for the Coalition at every state and federal election since turning eighteen. But he officially announces the end of his romance with ScoMo. "I have lost complete faith in the political system," he tells me. "Scott Morrison will go. But I don't know who to vote for."

The 2022 election will be like watching a larrikin in a pissing contest with his own shadow. The trick for Albanese has been convincing voters that *he* is the real Spartacus and not the bullshit artist. Initially, it seemed impossible to eclipse ScoMo, a masterpiece of working-class unpretentiousness. But by the 2022 election, voters might have got one too many glimpses of the smirk and shirk underneath the masquerade of mateship. "Christian" is the least offensive c-word used by a former cabinet colleague of Scott Morrison to describe the prime minister and his posse of Pentecostals.

"Morrison's clique is clever, calculating, cunning, conniving," says the senior Liberal figure. "That arrogance and authoritarianism has served them very well with journalists. But their time is coming. Labor might pull its finger out and win the election. And Australian politics will revert back to the centre more than where Morrison is very quietly taking it at the moment."

Jennifer Rayner

One of the more interesting parts of the Covid-19 era has been observing the ways people can and can't imagine our world will be different after this once-in-a-century crisis. Apparently cities, with their crowded CBDs and coop-like apartments, are over; the logistics and supply chains we've relied on for half a century will be radically reshaped; and the frontline work of carers will finally be valued in line with its social contribution (if only). But in George Megalogenis's *Exit Strategy: Politics after the Pandemic*, something that is not questioned is the primacy of the federal government in setting the direction for Australia's recovery and beyond – whether by commission or omission.

This is puzzling because, as Megalogenis notes, the story of the pandemic is the story of a federal government being absent when leadership was needed, slow and hesitant when speed and decisiveness were essential. Late in the essay he observes, "Morrison's approach has posed a question no one thought to ask before the pandemic: who actually runs the country? The answer in this crisis was the national cabinet, with the premiers claiming their greatest share of power in the federation since Whitlam commenced the long march of centralisation in the 1970s."

The essay treats this as a temporary state, with Megalogenis's thoughtful counsel being addressed to a federal government that is assumed to be back in the driver's seat. But there is another way to see it. Arguably, what the pandemic has really done is lay bare a progressive shift in power between levels of government that has been taking place since the fractious start of the Abbott–Turnbull–Morrison government. Looked at this way, what we've seen during the Covid crisis is not an aberration – it's a window into an alternative way to govern this country as we emerge from the pandemic.

As Megalogenis points out, in September 2021 the government will mark eight years in office, with the first five years being, "on its own admission, wasted." The rapid burn of leaders has prevented any policy idea or agenda from sticking for too long. Party-room dynamics and the scarring experience of the 2014 budget have tempered any appetite for complex reform. Pretty much the only flag all parts of the party have consistently been able to rally around is the idea of getting the federal budget back to surplus, necessitating a smallness of ambition and a reduced scope for government action in the name of "budget repair."

All this has created a vacuum: of ideas, of reform, of a willingness to face up to the hard challenges confronting Australia and actually do something about them. This vacuum is one that states and territories have increasingly been stepping into over the past eight years.

Australia lags the world on climate action, doesn't it? The federal government has refused to join other advanced economies in pursuing genuine emissions reduction, but it's happening anyway – because of the states and territories. In the past few years, all jurisdictions have signed up to achieve net-zero emissions by 2050 and are getting on with the hard change needed to achieve this. That includes both Labor *and* Liberal governments, which have realised that the window to act is closing and we can't keep playing politics while the world literally burns.

Today's politicians lack the guts to deliver real economy-shaping tax reform, don't they? Someone must have forgotten to tell that to Victoria, South Australia and New South Wales, which are all in the process of delivering road-user charging reforms that will address the long-term structural decline in federal fuel excise revenue, while helping to tackle emissions and congestion all in one handy tax. Or the ACT, which is well advanced in getting rid of stamp duty – a reform that the Henry Tax Review and approximately 4000 other experts believe is essential to improve productivity and equity in the housing market.

The states and territories have even demonstrated that near-national tax reform can be achieved through coordinated action. The introduction of point-of-consumption gaming taxes, capturing offshore betting operators, is a notable recent example, led by the South Australian government in 2017. All jurisdictions except the Northern Territory now have point-of-consumption taxes in place, tightening the tax net for an age of digital service delivery. The approach to developing these particular taxes was a case study in collaborative yet competitive federalism, with jurisdictions agreeing to create a broadly common tax base but leaving room to compete on the rate.

Australia is bound for gridlock and lost growth because we've failed to invest in infrastructure, right? Infrastructure Partnerships Australia tracks the Coalition's infrastructure spend since coming to office in 2014 at $50.2 billion, an average of about $7 billion a year. Over the same period, New South Wales, Victoria and Queensland alone spent $217 billion, or around four times as much per year. In fact, in every year of the Abbott–Turnbull–Morrison government, New South Wales *alone* has invested more in infrastructure than the federal government has across the entire country. To give credit where it's due, the Morrison government's last two budgets have significantly stepped up infrastructure spending, with a little over $40 billion earmarked for the next three years to 2024. But that investment is entirely dwarfed by the $140 *billion* that Australia's three largest states plan to spend on making their cities and regions more connected, efficient and productive over the same period.

All this is by way of demonstrating that the federal government's wasted years have been anything but for the states and territories. There are many more examples of these jurisdictions rolling up their sleeves and getting on with the job while Australia's media and commentariat have been preoccupied with the Coalition's successive unravellings and rebuildings. Important lessons have been learned in these years about how the states and territories can go it alone, together.

For example, they are increasingly working together through channels and forums that are completely independent of the federal government. This is a distinct operating shift from the hub-and-spoke model that dominated during the Rudd–Gillard government, where all roads led to Canberra. An important example of this is the Board of Treasurers, which exclusively comprises state and territory representatives. It was established by the NSW *Liberal* treasurer Dominic Perrottet as a forum for jurisdictions to debate and pursue economic reform. It has proven to be a welcome circuit-breaker on the interminable lemniscate conversations within the Commonwealth-controlled Council of Federal Financial Relations.

The strengthening of direct ties has also opened new opportunities for healthily competitive collaboration. This has seen states and territories learning from one another while also jockeying for position. On issues as diverse as tax, industry development, zero emissions transition, waste, mental health, hospitals, skills and energy, jurisdictions are looking over each other's fences for ideas and to benefit from the experience of governments that have tackled hard things first. While the federal government seems afraid to stick its neck out too far on anything at all, states and territories are increasingly making it a point of pride to be the first out of the gates and have other jurisdictions follow their example.

At the same time, the capability of the states and territories has been significantly boosted by an inflow of former federal public servants and advisers who believe in the power of government and want to wield it to drive real change. Regardless of your political persuasion, the Abbott–Turnbull–Morrison years have been an uninspiring time to work in government – dominated by messy and politicised decision-making processes, frequent policy reversals and a reticence to act on problems even when all the indicator lights are flashing red. Many workers have simply made the choice to take their skills elsewhere, strengthening state and territory governments with their knowledge, networks and larger frame of reference.

All this meant that Australia arguably entered the Covid-19 pandemic with the strongest states and territories and the weakest federal government for several decades. The collective action on display when premiers demanded a seat around the table at crisis HQ didn't materialise overnight. It was an expression of existing relationships and power dynamics six years in the making. The possibility that Megalogenis's essay missed is: what if we were to go forward like this, not back to the old world of centralised federal control?

This alternative would see the federal government take on the role of partner, not paterfamilias, to the states and territories. Vertical fiscal imbalance and the benefits of a national perspective will mean the federal government always has some role to play in guiding our collective future. But there's no reason the federal government needs to be the pre-eminent decision-maker on the post-pandemic economy and policy agenda. Jurisdictions would no doubt welcome an approach in which ends were collaboratively agreed, but each had more autonomy to decide on the means. While national consistency in policy has its merits, its pursuit has often also led to gridlock and paralysis, or lowest-common-denominator outcomes that don't end up moving the dial much. Being closer to communities, the states and territories may also choose to put different issues on the policy agenda than those the federal government has prioritised in recent years. It could only strengthen our democracy for citizens to feel that their concerns are being heard and acted upon.

In some ways this would mark a return to an earlier phase of the Australian federation, when the colonial states regularly muscled up to the nascent Commonwealth. But at the same time, it represents the kind of dispersed and flexible governance that is increasingly seen as necessary to meet the challenges of a world that is becoming more plural, more complex, and is demanding more innovation and experimentation.

If Australia ever gets around to having a credible national climate policy, it will need to be built around frameworks that are already in place and working across the states and territories. The next tax-reform agenda won't look like the last one, because the up-to-date expertise in designing and delivering complex reform sits in state treasuries and revenue offices, not a Commonwealth Treasury exhausted from the vast effort of keeping the economy together through Covid. More coordination on infrastructure, service delivery and post-recovery program design will be essential to avoid a repeat of the gaps and inefficiencies that the pandemic put up in lights.

The question, then, really is: will future federal governments go with the flow and share more power with states and territories that have shown themselves capable of wielding it well? Or will the coming decade be a fight by the feds to take back all the ground given away since 2014? These are not just questions for Scott Morrison's Coalition; federal Labor, too, will need to decide what sort of role it wants to play when its next prime minister fronts the premiers. With such a strong cast of experienced and popular state Labor leaders, it would be bold to think Anthony Albanese or anyone else could easily slip back into the old federal role.

Early in his essay, Megalogenis notes that "Covid-19 has demonstrated a wicked genius for exploiting gaps in the old model." He was talking about the economic model, but in fact the pandemic has laid bare gaps and fractures right across our society – including in how we are governed. The relationship of levels of Australian government may be a rare instance in which what has been exposed is actually an improvement on how we believed things were. We shouldn't therefore assume that the only way forward is back – back to centralised federal control, back to states and territories as the second tier by design and by function. To do so would be to miss an important opportunity to build a better system of government for our post-pandemic future.

Jennifer Rayner

Richard Denniss

Like most people, I do judge books by their covers, and so I was excited to read George Megalogenis's *Exit Strategy: Politics after the Pandemic*. Like many, I have been thinking a lot about "Where to from here?" when it comes to policy, politics and democracy itself.

In the introduction, I was excited to read that the essay's "aim is to identify those parts of the old model that are irredeemably broken and to provide a new answer to the question of what government should be responsible for in the twenty-first century."

Alas, while I learned a lot about the ideological shifts of recent decades and a lot about the machinations of the National Cabinet, Treasury and the Treasurer, I feel I missed out on what was promised on the cover. I wanted a lot more on possible exit strategies and the political forces that will determine which options are placed on the democratic menu and, ultimately, which dish is selected.

But now that I'm hungry for such answers, let me try to fill the void I created for myself. Let's start with the big picture. The Australian economy didn't "snap back" from the devastation of Covid-19, it was dragged back to safety by an enormous injection of welfare spending, resuscitated with a huge dose of public-sector infrastructure spending, industry assistance and cheap credit from the Reserve Bank. It remains on life support today, thanks to forecast budget deficits of over $50 billion per year for all of the out-years in the federal budget. Remember when Tony Abbott thought a budget deficit of $18 billion constituted a "budget emergency"? And remember when the media and business took him seriously?

The parts of the old model that are "irredeemably broken" are the ideas that the Liberals have an aversion to budget deficits and, more significantly, that the size of the budget deficit is a meaningful indicator of economic management. The "policy elite" in Australia has fetishised budget surpluses for decades, but this fetish is almost exclusively Australian. The last US president to deliver a budget surplus was Bill Clinton and the last UK prime minister to do so was Tony Blair. I hope this crisis will kill off an idea that thirty years of data from nearly 200 countries has been unable to euthanise.

Relatedly, it's important to note that Australia's economic recovery wasn't gas-led, investment-led or private sector–led – it was entirely led by government spending. And it worked. For decades, Australians have been told not only that budget deficits are bad, but also that government spending is both inherently inefficient and a poor way to boost an economy heading into recession. George quotes former Treasury secretary Ken Henry saying this hostility to government spending "was not something that the Australian Treasury had dreamt up … The academic consensus around fiscal policy was basically: 'It's too hard to use' … the best thing to do is sit on your hands and let the private sector work it out."

What utter crap. No such academic consensus ever existed, and it's not at all clear from the essay whether George believes it did. But what is clear – if we are considering the irredeemably broken aspects of the old model – is the tendency in Australia for powerful people to source advice, economic or otherwise, from those they agree with. It is simply absurd to suggest that Ken Henry or his successor Martin Parkinson, who was also interviewed for the essay, could not find academic economists who thought that activist fiscal policy was a good idea. They simply didn't think those economists were worth talking to. Luckily for millions of Australians who benefited from JobKeeper and the JobSeeker supplement, the current secretary of Treasury, Steven Kennedy, who wasn't interviewed for the essay, has clearly paid a lot more attention to the diversity of opinion among the world's economists. But despite the radical, and desirable, shift in Treasury's views about fiscal policy, few, if any, of our "policy elite" have owned up to the enormity of their errors over the past thirty years. It's a pity the essay treats them all so gently.

Also broken irredeemably by Covid-19 was the idea that the success of the private sector is separable from the effectiveness of the public sector. While Treasury, the Coalition and neoliberal policy elite talk about public spending "crowding out" private-sector activity, the opposite has just been shown to be the case. Without the (second-rate) publicly owned NBN to help businesses pivot rapidly to online services, and without the publicly owned Australia Post to deliver more than 2 million parcels a day, the "free market" could not have received or dispatched most of its orders. Does anyone think that a privatised Australia Post would have doubled its parcel capacity during the crisis? Or would the private owners have simply trebled their prices?

But imagine if our NBN weren't crap. And imagine if Australia Post hadn't been scaling back its services in regional areas for years. A bigger, better public sector would have helped both Australian businesses and Australian communities get through the Covid crisis in even better shape. Ironically, while there's no evidence that income tax cuts to those earning $200,000 "trickle down" to help small business and regional Australia, there's overwhelming evidence that high-quality public services do. Evidence that Treasury and the academics they preferred to talk to systematically ignored.

But let's take it further. Imagine if more kids in low-income households had laptops to use for their home schooling because Kevin Rudd's free laptop program had been maintained. And imagine if our run-down and privatised aged-care system wasn't (under)staffed by hard working casuals who are often under-trained, under-supported and have to work across multiple sites to earn a living wage? We could have got through the Covid crisis more productively and more safely if our public sector had been bigger and better. Public spending is not inherently inefficient and wasteful – when it is well targeted, it has huge positives, but when it is used to reward friends and buy votes, it delivers inequality.

The fact that far more people died in privatised aged care than in publicly run centres should irredeemably break the idea that outsourced and privatised services are more efficient than publicly run ones, but it probably won't. I wish George had spent more time considering why that is the case. Even before Covid-19 hit, the royal commissions into aged care, disability care and the banks had made a mockery of Treasury's delusional view that privatisation and deregulation would drive efficiency and productivity growth while providing higher-quality care to vulnerable Australians.

Let me now turn to the second part of George's question: what lessons from the past can guide us in the future?

The lengthy restatement of the failings of the Rudd government's pink batts scheme is a useful reminder that when a government "outsources" the delivery of a service it can and should be held responsible for the results. But why, ten years after the abolition of the scheme that tragically cost four lives, does it remain the media's go-to example of government failure?

The Coalition is currently spending $10,000 per day per asylum seeker detained by private contractors on Nauru, and Australia is estimated to have spent more than $7 billion on offshore detention since 2012. If the very fact of the Royal Commission into Violence, Abuse, Neglect and Exploitation of People with Disability isn't shocking enough, the evidence it heard should be enough to shame someone into resignation for "overseeing" the creation of our "deregulated" system. But it hasn't, and nor has the harrowing evidence the commission heard, including the tragic case of Ms Ann-Marie Smith, who "lived with cerebral palsy and at the time of her death was found to be suffering, among other things, septic shock, multiple organ failure, severe pressure sores and malnutrition."

Just read that again and ask yourself how "efficient" the market is in providing care to vulnerable Australians.

Sure, the pink batts scheme was poorly designed and implemented, but unlike our outsourced and privatised "care" of asylum seekers, the disabled and the elderly, with all of its expensive horrors, the pink batts scheme was scrapped. No one is talking about scrapping the private provision of care for the vulnerable in Australia. The same bureaucracy that oversaw the "disaster" of the pink batts scheme had no qualms about pretending quality would be high and rorting would be low when it designed the outsourced and privatised National Disability Insurance Scheme.

In the section of his essay entitled "Slow Learners," George applauds Treasury for eventually learning that Keynesian economics both exists and is effective, but he is silent on the fact that it is yet to admit that its preference for privatised service delivery has killed a lot of people, ruined a lot of lives and wasted a mountain of money. Even the chair of the ACCC is now calling for a halt to privatisations if governments can't figure out how to regulate the private monopolies they keep selling off.

While George doesn't answer the question of what government should do in the remaining three-quarters of the twenty-first century, I think stopping publicly funded but privately owned companies from ripping off the most vulnerable Australians should be at the top of the list. But what other problems should our national state turn its mind to, now that Treasury and the rest of us know that budget deficits aren't scary, that public-sector infrastructure allows private-sector innovation to occur, and that outsourcing is more likely to increase fraud than efficiency?

Here's a start:

How can governments protect our privacy in the age of big data?

How can governments protect freedom of speech and diversity of opinion as social media and traditional media merge into a form of power that was unimaginable just twenty years ago?

As the UK renationalises its rail system after its failed privatisation, what assets might the Australian government renationalise?

If we can spend $10 billion each year subsidising fossil fuels, why can't we spend $10 billion each year on renewable energy?

If Telstra can make all calls from pay phones free, what other services might Australian governments provide for free in Australia? Wi-fi? Drinking water? Air-conditioned workspaces to help people study and work from home? Public housing?

While George's essay has a considered analysis of climate change, it doesn't discuss which bits of the old model climate change has broken (including the pretence that Liberals prefer market-based solutions) or how it will reshape the role of the public sector. Who will insure houses in disaster-prone regions? Where will poor people go to escape extreme heat?

We now know that the benefits of low wages, low taxes and low job security don't trickle down to the poor — instead they literally get blasted off into space. So what will we in "the land of the fair go" do about wealth and income inequality, now that even the IMF and World Bank admit that income inequality is a brake on economic growth?

While neoliberalism led the Australian policy elite to make lots of mistakes in the way they handled recessions, the way they worried about government spending and the way they privatised so many services and business, the biggest mistake that flows from neoliberalism isn't how small it makes our government, but how small it makes our imaginations.

When our self-anointed policy elite believe that "market forces" will fix all of our problems, they absolve themselves of the hard task of fixing anything. Indeed, they spend their time fighting people like me, who think that government might be able to make some people's lives bigger and better. And while they obsess over the cost of being a bit nicer to the unemployed, they turn a blind eye to spending $7 billion to be a lot nastier to asylum seekers.

The saddest, most embarrassing part of the Australian policy debate over the past thirty years isn't that it took so long to realise that no one else in the world cared about our budget surplus, or that so many of Australia's policy elite still hark back to the "golden years" of the 1980s and 1990s when looking for a "reform agenda"; it's that, even now, Australia — the fourteenth-biggest economy in the world, a member of the OECD, the G20 and the Five Eyes intelligence alliance — is waiting to hear from overseas thinkers and politicians what its post-Covid future might look like. How pathetic.

Australia was once at the forefront of so many important reforms. No, I don't mean Paul Keating selling the Commonwealth Bank, or John Howard's big shift from sales tax to the GST — I mean women's suffrage, electing the world's first labour government and the creation of a system of centralised wage-fixing.

When Australia was much smaller, much poorer and much more tied to Mother England, our leaders showed far more independence, creativity and resolve than they do today. But perhaps that was neoliberalism's best trick: convincing Australians that "the world" and "the market" would shape our destiny, not our own ideas, courage and determination.

My favourite sentence in George's essay is: "The power of neoliberalism was never in its observance by conservatives but its effect on the other party." In my Quarterly Essay, *Dead Right*, I tried to argue the other side of the same coin: that those on the right never really took neoliberalism seriously, but rather used it as a rhetorical excuse to cut spending on their enemies and cut taxes on their friends.

George quotes the magical words that John Howard allegedly shared with Josh Frydenberg at the beginning of the Covid-19 crisis: "In times of crisis there are no ideological constraints." But unfortunately, like nearly everyone, he misses the joke. There never are, and never have been, "ideological constraints" on the ability of the Liberal Party to spend other people's money on their friends. The IMF said that Peter Costello was the most profligate treasurer in Australian history, and Tony Abbott's hysteria about a "budget emergency" didn't stop him introducing income tax cuts.

I think there is a way out of neoliberalism's disaster zones. I know there must be, as most countries don't have them. I think the Covid crisis provides a unique opportunity to begin that search, but unfortunately, while I learned a lot reading George's essay, I didn't find the exit strategy I was looking for.

Richard Denniss

Dennis Altman

The difficulty with writing about current events is that they change faster than it takes to produce and circulate an essay. I am writing this during Sydney's Covid-induced lockdown, which has shattered the myth that the New South Wales government could manage the epidemic more successfully than the other states, even as it reinforces George's argument about the fracturing of the federation.

Where George's essay is strongest is in its assessment of the shifting political landscape of party loyalties and the Coalition's hostility to universities, which he sees as connected. He is correct that state allegiances have changed, particularly that of Victoria, once the jewel in Menzies' Liberal Party and now the strongest Labor state. But there seems to be some confusion in his argument, which shifts between suggesting that political fault lines lie along state lines and that there is a city–country divide.

Massive swings against Labor in regional Queensland at the last election certainly reflected perceptions that Labor is hostile to coalmining, but this hardly explains Labor's failure to win back seats in suburban areas of the capital cities. While Labor seems obsessed with winning back coastal Queensland seats, it could easily win government if the five metropolitan areas of Australia voted similarly to Melbourne. Of the ten most marginal government seats following the last election, all but three are in the capital cities, and those three include electorates in Cairns and Launceston, neither of which depends on mining.

Only in Melbourne and Adelaide does Labor hold a clear majority of seats; Sydney, once reliably Labor south of the harbour, is now fairly equally divided. That Sydney has become much more culturally conservative than Melbourne is suggested by the results of the plebiscite on marriage equality in 2019. Of the ten electorates that recorded the highest "no" vote, eight were in Sydney, with only one (Maranoa) in rural Australia.

George suggests that the Coalition's hostility to universities is closely related to Morrison's apparent disregard for Victoria. Yes, the major export industry of

Victoria has become higher education, while New South Wales' is coal, but it is unlikely that this is a major factor explaining votes in metropolitan Sydney. Josh Frydenberg claims universities are victims of their own success, citing their willingness to embrace a corporate model, but he saw no problem in allowing major corporations to access JobKeeper and JobSaver programs, which were denied to universities. Given there are well over a million local university students in Australia, one would have thought the electoral calculus alone would encourage governments to be more supportive.

The consequences of declining financial support for universities are severe, not only for staff who lose jobs and students who can expect declining support. After the University of Western Australia, one of the richest universities in the country, embarked on a round of midyear cuts, Professor Mark Beeson pointed out that the cuts would drastically reduce the number of people working in the areas of international affairs and the politics and societies of the Indo-Pacific, with Asian Studies becoming further marginalised, Other universities have seen major cutbacks in language programs, including major Asian language programs.

Governments of both persuasions are obsessed with the need for more science and technology students, but in a complex and threatening global environment there is an equal need to increase competencies in disciplines associated with international studies. If, as the Morrison government believes, China presents a major long-term threat to Australia's security, there should be a greater emphasis on building deep ties with the countries of Southeast Asia and expanding Australia's diplomatic footprint, which is smaller than that of other countries of comparable wealth. One detects in Morrison something of an echo of Tony Abbott's obsession with "the Anglosphere," and a failure to recognise the long-term damage of successive cuts in foreign assistance to regions other than the Pacific.

The key question is whether either side of politics has the skills and vision to guide Australia into a post-pandemic world. One of the consequences of the pandemic has been an emphasis on the role of government; the neoliberal panacea of letting the market rip is no longer attractive, as George indicates. Sadly, the lack of a vision for the future is largely bipartisan; having been scared off by the reaction to Shorten's mild suggestions for correcting some of the rorts within our taxation system, the current Labor Party finds itself unable to argue for the increased government commitments needed to improve our health, education and welfare systems. At a moment that calls for radical innovation, Labor risks missing the opportunity to offer a genuine alternative to the lack of imagination which George so accurately points to in the Morrison government.

Dennis Altman

Tanya Plibersek

George Megalogenis's central argument in *Exit Strategy* feels particularly prescient this week, as I work from home and argue with my kids about their remote learning. It's hard to disagree that, while Australia might have handled the original Covid-19 crisis well, we're badly fumbling our transition out of it.

When we needed federal leadership to secure and deliver vaccines, our prime minister was slow and stubborn. When we needed national coordination to fix our quarantine system, he stuck his head in the sand. Now, eighteen months into the pandemic, we're all paying for his complacency.

But the failure of leadership goes beyond the immediate situation. It is impossible to discern Mr Morrison's plan for social and economic recovery after the pandemic. Indeed, instead of planning for a better normal after Covid-19, the Morrison government seems content to snap back to low wages, insecure work and growing inequality. And it is using Covid-19 as a cover to settle old scores.

The most obvious and destructive example is universities. As Megalogenis writes, "given the gargantuan sums being borrowed and spent on the safety net, no one needed to be worse off. Yet the Morrison government chose to exclude universities from JobKeeper." And just to make clear this wasn't an accident, Scott Morrison changed the JobKeeper rules three times to ensure unis were left out.

This decision has led to tens of thousands of jobs being lost – in our cities, in our suburbs and in our regional areas. It's led to the University of Western Australia closing its sociology and anthropology schools. It's led to the ANU almost dissolving its neuroscience department. It's led to Swinburne University discontinuing all foreign language courses and the University of Newcastle cancelling more than 500 courses and degrees in engineering, creative industries and computer science. It's led to campuses closing in Biloela and Yeppoon, and it's led to significant job losses. More than 30,000 jobs have been lost across Sydney, Melbourne, Bendigo, Geelong, Rockhampton, Adelaide and Perth.

At first glance, this might look puzzling. When the pandemic began, higher education was Australia's fourth-largest export industry. It was almost double the size of the next largest services export – tourism – which did receive JobKeeper and much-needed additional assistance. Universities employ more than 200,000 Australians across a spectrum of jobs: professors, scientists, librarians, cafeteria workers, cleaners, admin assistants and gardeners.

Universities are teaching the nurses, doctors, scientists and epidemiologists who will fight the next pandemic. The world-class research conducted in universities will help us sequence the next virus genome, discover the next vaccine and solve the public health conundrum of vaccine hesitancy. Academics – our scientists, social scientists and many others – have been on television every night helping us interpret the scientific, public health, economic and workplace impacts of the pandemic.

So why sabotage such a source of national wealth and safety?

As an anonymous government figure admits in the essay, "It's not that complicated. The government hates universities." And that's what we're dealing with here: an irrational, ideological crusade against higher education in Australia. It's not about costs and benefits – it's about enemies and vengeance.

We should be building a better integrated higher education system, in which people can mix and match the qualifications they need from an equitable, world-class system of universities and TAFEs, and in which both universities and TAFE are supported, promoted and funded to expand their complex, specialised work. Instead the government wants to drive a wedge between vocational and university education – to pretend that university is for the "latte-sipping elites" and that real, salt-of-the-earth Australians go to TAFE.

Thankfully, most Australians don't share the modern conservative antipathy towards universities. The Liberals' lazy stereotypes don't stand up to reality, partly because democratising access to university was a big success. We're not talking about a small and exclusive club here. In Australia, over 40 per cent of people aged twenty-five to forty now hold a bachelor's degree. Working-class parents, like mine, certainly don't resent their kids going to university. They take pride in it.

The only people who do resent universities – who want Australians to be split into warring camps, supporting either university or TAFE – are the Liberal politicians trying to engineer a cheap culture war. (Of course, that never stopped them going to university themselves. Every single Liberal Party cabinet minister responsible for withholding JobKeeper was a university graduate, and the minister who doubled the cost of humanities courses holds three separate humanities degrees.)

The simple fact is if you're building a bridge, you need an architect and an engineer, as well as a concrete formworker and a plumber. And you may just need a humanities graduate to deal with community concerns about increased traffic, or to model who may benefit from new infrastructure and who may miss out. Our economy needs strong and excellent universities, just as it needs a strong and excellent TAFE system.

Supporting universities is a matter of rewarding individual aspiration. There remains a "graduate premium" on earning. Over their lifetimes, men with a degree earn $800,000 more on average. Women earn $600,000 more. Why would any government want to deny that opportunity to its citizens?

But the benefit of a university education goes well beyond the individual. For every dollar spent on higher education, there is a 200 to 300 per cent public return on investment for the whole community. The drop in Australian university exports during Covid has seen the Australian economy lose an estimated $18 billion, in one year alone. The failure of the federal government to invest properly in universities and research over the coming years will cost the Australian economy more still.

We know that productivity growth in Australia has been pathetic in recent years. Our economy needs highly skilled graduates, just as it needs the discoveries of our world-class researchers. The Australian economy has a worryingly narrow base. In global rankings of economic complexity, we're languishing in the eighty-seventh spot. That puts us between Uganda and Burkina Faso – and dead last in the OECD. With most of our eggs in a handful of export baskets, we're more vulnerable to changes in commodity prices or to a trading partner turning its back on us suddenly.

We need world-class university research to help diversify our economy, to generate new local industries and to drive long-term growth. All international evidence points in the same direction: the more skilled and educated a country is, the more prosperous it will be. This makes the government's decision to trash our universities all the more baffling – and all the more infuriating.

Luckily, there's a different model available to us. Past leaders have chosen to invest in our education system, particularly in moments of crisis.

A lot of attention has been given this year to Australia's reconstruction policies after World War II. John Curtin and Ben Chifley's ambitious program, built around full employment and mass housing, shines like a beacon for our own recovery. Their Labor governments managed to defeat the immediate threat of the war, while building something better for the future.

What might be less known is the role that universities played in post-war reconstruction. The war was a complex operation, which taught our federal leaders the important lesson that we desperately needed more skilled graduates and more technical expertise in Australia.

Our leaders responded with an unprecedented expansion of Commonwealth investment in universities. They built the Australian National University. They doubled Commonwealth research grants. They wrote a new act for the CSIRO. They established the Commonwealth Reconstruction Training Scheme, Australia's version of the American GI Bill, which paid the tuition of 60,000 returned servicemen and women.

Robert Menzies was also one of the fathers of higher education in Australia. Along with Curtin and Chifley, he helped build the modern university system – and set it on its first steps towards democratisation. Funnily enough, Menzies' only hesitation was bringing technical subjects into the traditional university. "We must never forget," he insisted, "that the university's function was to educate individuals in culture and learning and not to create technical experts."

It was Labor that argued for the inclusion of technical degrees such as engineering in the university system. It was Labor, led by Gough Whitlam, that opened up universities, seeing working-class people, including many women, obtain degrees for the first time. It was Labor, led by Bob Hawke, that helped establish technology universities such as UTS and RMIT.

This is the agenda we should be replicating and modernising, geared to the needs of a post-pandemic world. Young Australians who are prepared to study hard after their year (or years) from hell as remote-learning students should be rewarded with a place at university or TAFE that will help them win the job of their dreams. Mature-age students wanting to advance in their career, or change their career altogether, should have the chance to do that too. Price should never shut people out of an education.

Employers should be able to find the qualified staff they need in Australia, especially in a world where international borders remain uncertain. We should be able to take Australian inventiveness and build businesses from our discoveries and innovation, creating jobs and diversifying our economy. We should put our best minds to work on solving problems for the benefit of humanity.

As I wrote in my book Upturn last year, "In a democracy, government is a vehicle for collective problem-solving. If we can't solve the social and economic problems facing us today, we will see a continuing decline in people's faith in democracy itself."

We have no shortage of problems to solve together, and universities have a critical role to play in finding those solutions. The government's overt hostility to higher education can only be explained by a determination to hoard the benefits of education and deny the utility of learning, research, discovery, innovation, question and challenge. We will all be poorer for it.

Tanya Plibersek

Andrew Norton

Since Australia's borders closed in March 2020, preventing new international students from enrolling onshore in Australian universities, the government has made higher education policy errors. At this high level of generality, I agree with George Megalogenis in *Exit Strategy*. But I would like to present a different analysis of events since, and to share the blame more broadly.

Like many in the higher education sector, George Megalogenis argues that "denying" universities access to JobKeeper was a mistake. But JobKeeper was never the solution to the problems universities face. The program suited businesses that could recover swiftly once Covid restrictions lifted, taking back their old workforces to serve customers newly freed from home detention. It wasn't right for universities, which face a prolonged decline before a slow recovery.

The first Covid lockdowns created an immediate cashflow problem for many Australian businesses. Financial problems developed more slowly for universities. After a fast move to online teaching, they delivered most of their scheduled classes to most of their expected first-semester 2020 students. Direct travel from China stopped on 1 February, stranding some Chinese students overseas, but fortunately many of them studied online. With a few exceptions, first-semester international students from other countries arrived before all routine international travel ended in the second half of March. But with the borders still closed, midyear international student intakes fell well below previous years.

Financial results in university annual reports confirm that 2020 revenue declines were contained. For the thirty-five universities with published 2020 annual reports as of late July 2021, total revenue was down 5.3 per cent on 2019 levels. A slight increase in government grant and HELP student-loan income partly offset reduced fee income.

The federal government did tighten university JobKeeper criteria to make universities less likely to qualify. But university annual reports suggest that few would have satisfied the rules applying to other organisations. Their loss of revenue just wasn't large enough.

Rather than the quick dip and rapid recovery envisaged by JobKeeper, universities face accumulating financial problems caused by long-term border closures. As of May 2021, commencing international enrolments were a third lower than those of the same period in 2019. Although that may sound better than expected, the enrollees are students who were already in Australia. As time goes on, the number of potential international students who arrived before March 2020 will dwindle.

Losses against pre-Covid revenue projections will continue growing past mid-2022, when borders are expected to reopen. Someone who is not a first-year student in 2021 will not be a second-year student in 2022, and so on. It will take years to rebuild total numbers and fee income.

Under this scenario, a JobKeeper-style policy to keep all employees and employers together is not feasible. It would mean keeping staff on the payroll to teach students who won't be back for years, and whose enrolments are not vulnerable only to Covid-19 or Australian border policies. China might stop its citizens studying here, changes to visa rules may deter prospective Indian students, or our competitors could gain lasting market shares while Australia remains a hermit nation.

Some jobs could be preserved by teaching more domestic students, and the government allocated $550 million in temporary funding for additional domestic student places, mostly in short graduate-certificate courses. But the unmet demand for domestic student places is well below the numbers of lost international students.

The university business model means that retrenchments reach way beyond staff directly involved in international education. Profits on international students have financed many otherwise unaffordable university activities. On my estimates, these profits funded at least $3.3 billion of the $12 billion that universities spent on research in 2018, and quite possibly much more.

Although the 21st-century university research boom is clearly over, an orderly phase-down of research activity would avoid projects being closed prior to completion, with all the waste that would involve. It only gets a passing sentence in *Exit Strategy*, but the government did provide an additional $1 billion in research funding for 2021.

The problem is that no additional research money, and only a small amount of temporary student-places funding, will continue into 2022, which is likely to be the peak year of the Covid crisis in higher education. That was a significant omission in the May 2021 budget.

In explaining these and other absent dollars, *Exit Strategy* pursues two arguments, around educational spending priorities and voting patterns.

According to *Exit Strategy*'s account, since John Howard's term as prime minister, Coalition governments have pursued a dubious long-term strategy to preference private-school funding over public-university funding. The essay says that the Whitlam, Fraser, Hawke and Keating governments never considered giving more money to private schools than universities.

At one level, it would not be surprising if private-school funding surpassed university funding, as private-school enrolments exceed domestic higher education student numbers by more than 200,000. But the poor presentation of higher education assistance in Budget Paper No. 1, which looks like the source of *Exit Strategy*'s numbers, obscures much of the Commonwealth's funding.

According to Budget Paper No. 1, non-government school funding in 2021–22 is $14.7 billion, while higher education funding is put at $10.6 billion. The budget documents don't explain this, but the $10.6 billion consists of grants authorised by the *Higher Education Support Act 2003*. It omits funding from the annual appropriations bill, along with money authorised under separate legislation for the Australian Research Council and the National Health and Medical Research Council. It doesn't include higher education student income support or HELP student loans. The budget papers do not itemise all funding sources according to sector, but I estimate that total Commonwealth cash outlays for higher education purposes will be approximately $22 billion in 2021–22. HELP repayments will probably be around $4 billion, leaving $18 billion in net cash outlays – more than the Budget Paper No. 1 figure for non-government schools.

University and private-school funding are similar in the ways they fit into the Australian system of funding social services. Both mix public and private funding; private schools have done so since the late 1960s, and universities have always done so, although there were no domestic higher education student tuition charges between 1974 and 1988. In both sectors, the government means-tests public contributions, although in novel ways, using parental income for schools and graduate income for higher education students via the HELP repayment system.

Despite the similarities in their funding models, their political circumstances differ. Like George Megalogenis in *Exit Strategy*, many people who support more funding for public universities see something wrong with funding private schools. The Coalition, on the other hand, sees a bigger and more sympathetic constituency in private schools than universities. Neither major political party believes that many votes turn on higher education policy.

Despite this political calculation, public universities, overall, did as well or better than private schools in the government's Covid response. Both were excluded from the JobKeeper registered-charity category, and were therefore required to demonstrate a revenue decline of at least 30 rather than 15 per cent to qualify for payments. The fact that both sectors receive significant Commonwealth funding already is the common factor, meaning that sector-specific mechanisms of support already existed, if needed. Some private schools did nevertheless qualify for JobKeeper. No public university received JobKeeper in its own right, although thirteen had subsidiaries that did.

Private schools could receive their government grants early, forgoing future income, while public universities could keep their teaching grant money, even if their domestic enrolments fell. Universities could retain previously budgeted HELP student-loan revenue, to be repaid between 2022 and 2029 if not matched by student borrowing. Private schools could also benefit from modest cash payments available for small businesses and not-for-profits, but there was nothing like the extra $1 billion in university research funding for private schools. But nor should there have been, as this money responded to a problem unique to universities.

We are left trying to explain why this research money does not continue into 2022. Limited and fractured advocacy from the sector itself may be a factor. Throughout the Covid crisis, it has, at least in public, offered few specific suggestions about how the government should respond. This may reflect the sector's diversity of interests. The research money mostly helped the research-intensive sandstone universities, and outside the Group of Eight lobby group, support for another year of it may have been lukewarm.

On the government's side, it may feel that it did not get a political dividend for its first $1 billion. This was partly its own fault; it revealed the funding in the very busy October 2020 budget rather than announcing it in the preceding weeks. But while the higher education interest groups acknowledge the significance of the funding, the broader higher education community reaction matches *Exit Strategy*'s. The additional money might be mentioned briefly, only to be reframed as a cut when future funding drops back to previously announced levels, before returning the discussion to grievances about JobKeeper, an unsuitable scheme now closed to everyone.

Higher education is never going win votes for the Liberal Party, but this does not mean the party won't respond to persuasive analyses of policy issues in the sector. There was a significant Covid response, albeit with the major elements of that response announced late in 2020 and finishing too early. The Job-Ready

Graduates policy, released in June 2020, which was unrelated to Covid issues, jeopardises courses and campuses with reduced per-student funding in some disciplines, and needlessly adds many years to HELP repayment times for some students. But Job-Ready Graduates should deliver more student places for the "Costello baby boom" cohort, who will reach university age in the mid-2020s.

On both sides, the government and the higher education community, there is room for more engagement, so that the next few years have fewer avoidable policy and political mistakes than the past few years.

Andrew Norton

Michael Wesley

Exit Strategy amply demonstrates why George Megalogenis sits at the top of Australia's small group of must-read columnists. Deep historical knowledge, sharp statistical analysis and an eye for the telling detail are woven elegantly together in a searching critique of the Australian political system's response to the Covid pandemic.

Covid has highlighted many hitherto vaguely apparent features of modern Australia, but perhaps none so starkly as the deep antipathy of many Australians towards universities. Megalogenis points this out when he says, "Perhaps the better question is not what motivated the rough treatment of higher education in a pandemic, but why the government doesn't fear a community backlash from a policy that appears to be based on prejudice, not evidence." The answer to that question is that the government is very aware that large parts of the electorate share its antipathy towards the universities.

Megalogenis's views on why this antipathy exists are interesting and possibly part of the answer, but do not go anywhere near providing a complete explanation. One of his views is that it is a generational issue: the government has channelled money away from universities towards private schools, because private-school parents are more likely to be Coalition voters, whereas uni students are more likely to vote Labor. The other is that it is a geographic issue: Melbourne, the "nominal capital of our universities and research institutions," is no longer as central in deciding elections as it was in Menzies' day.

Clues to more profoundly important reasons for anti-university attitudes are sprinkled through Megalogenis's account. Treasurer Josh Frydenberg tells him that when the pandemic hit, universities "had become very corporatised. They had relied very heavily on international students so they had shifted their business model over time. We were willing to provide very significant support for the universities, but they also had to adjust as other businesses did." This is a remarkable statement from a Liberal treasurer who holds Menzies' old seat.

Megalogenis points out forensically that government funding for universities has fallen steadily for over twenty years, even as more Australians have accessed university education each year. The "business model" adopted by Australian universities has allowed them to provide world-class education to greater numbers of Australians while relying less and less on the taxpayer. "Ordinarily," observes Megalogenis, "a conservative government would applaud the initiative and congratulate itself on the market response it had engineered. But … that success made the Coalition envious."

Many in the university sector are genuinely flummoxed as to why their success in raising export revenue is a problem, whereas miners' and farmers' export successes are lauded as a source of pride and national prosperity. It would be a huge missed opportunity if Australia's universities simply shake their heads and assume it's all about ideology. There are big questions to ask here. Why does a sector that is so economically important, that directly touches the lives of millions of Australians and that punches so far above our national weight in international rankings, have so few defenders beyond its campuses? Why this resentment, rather than admiration or gratitude or even respect? I suspect that while other similar countries have their anti-university voices, and many more invest heavily in universities as keys to future success, Australia is unique in the depth and breadth of its antipathy towards its universities.

But there are big questions for the government and the country also. Megalogenis points out that budget forecasts will see an absolute fall in university funding up to 2023–24. With borders remaining closed until mid-2022, international student revenues will fall as well. Meanwhile, demand for university education among Australians is surging. Unless the government puts aside its resentment and thinks clearly about the consequences, the "adjustment" Frydenberg called for must come in one or more of three areas. Most likely, more university job cuts will come. Australian students alarmed at increasing class sizes ain't seen nothin' yet. Or our world-class research capabilities will see their resources dwindle. Just as other countries are doubling down on education and research-driven transformations of their economies, Australia will see the atrophy of its knowledge economy. Or taxpayers will be hit to support the teaching of greater numbers of Australians. Perhaps Frydenberg and education minister Alan Tudge can explain to the country which part of this business model is in the national interest.

Michael Wesley

Travers McLeod

Reading Exit Strategy as most of Australia went back into lockdown with one of the world's worst vaccination rates made me wonder whether the title was an oxymoron.

When historians examine Australia's response to Covid-19, the absence of a clear strategy to steer Australia beyond a pandemic into a brighter future may well be the most mystifying part of the whole episode. Our inability to plan and implement a response to a known systemic risk could be one of the biggest own goals in our nation's history. If repeated on climate change, we are doomed to fail.

None of this discounts George Megalogenis's essay, which offers a dose of history on how Australia has tackled systemic shocks, the latest of which is Covid-19. His story of the distinctive values and culture of Australia's public services and the widespread acceptance that they should be able to offer frank professional advice without fear of losing their jobs provided a ray of light in an otherwise grim time, as did his snapshot of the new lease of life in Joe Biden's America, where strengthened social infrastructure and a US$450 billion investment in early childhood development are central tenets of the response.

Australian policymakers have known about the devastating regularity of pandemics for some time, and they were warned about the risk of coronaviruses specifically nearly a decade ago. A Senate Estimates hearing in federal parliament way back in June 2013 was told the possibility of a "novel coronavirus" was "very scary." Among the participants in that exchange was Jane Halton, then secretary of the Department of Health, who was appointed to the National Covid-19 Coordination Commission (NCCC) in March 2020 and was a key adviser as Australia explored suitable vaccines.

When the prime minister established the NCCC, he said it would "coordinate advice to the Australian government on actions to anticipate and mitigate the economic and social effects of the global coronavirus pandemic." This was, he said, "about mobilising a whole-of-society and whole-of-economy effort." The NCCC sounded like a "red team" for Covid-19, and it should have been, yet by 3 May 2021 its work had concluded. "We have moved past the emergency phase of the Covid-19 response and are now on the path of economic recovery," said the prime minister. "Australia's strong health and economic circumstances and our strong outlook make it the right time for the Board to conclude its work." With Australia then at the bottom of global vaccination rates, and the Delta strain having just been used to justify a ban on Australians returning from India, it beggars belief the NCCC was told to down tools early. One wonders what it actually did, or whether it offered nothing other than smoke and mirrors. Whatever the NCCC spent time on, it does not appear to have war-gamed different strategies on quarantine hubs or vaccination rollouts, or to have tested various tactics to keep Australia one step ahead of the virus.

The grim short story of Covid for Australia is that we were caught napping at the start and have been reactive throughout. While some of our responses have been inspired, overall we have lacked the courage and creativity to use the crisis to imagine a better future for Australians and our region. The initial flurry of national collaboration that we saw at the beginning of the outbreak has been replaced by a fractured federation. According to the Oxford Covid-19 Government Response Tracker, Australia now has some of the most stringent restrictions among OECD countries. That is a predictable consequence of sticking with last year's strategy, not chasing and securing multiple vaccines, being too slow to add new technologies to our arsenal, such as rapid lateral flow tests, and not preparing effectively for the inevitable future waves and variants.

Megalogenis is spot-on about Australians placing their faith in government being the story of the pandemic. I am willing to believe the desire Australians have for more active government was growing before Covid-19. Two years ago, in the Quarterly Essay *Australia Fair*, Rebecca Huntley wrote that Australia is a nation of democrats. The Centre for Policy Development's research on public attitudes reinforced this, revealing that, as Australians, we share a unique resolve to make democracy work, solve big problems and improve the lives of others. The 2019 federal election did not disprove Huntley's thesis. The twin crises since, the bushfires and pandemic, have put it firmly back in the frame. When CPD asked Australians in June 2020 what the main purpose of their democracy is, the answer three times more popular than any other was ensuring all people are treated fairly and equally, including the most vulnerable. This answer was chosen by 45 per cent of respondents, up from 36 per cent in 2018, far ahead of other answers, such as ensuring people are free to decide how to live (15 per cent) or electing representatives to make decisions (13 per cent).

The other key takeaway from this attitudes research was how voters across the political spectrum are at the end of their tether with the contracting-out services. On this, Australians are united. Ninety per cent now think it is important for government to maintain the capability and skills to deliver services directly, instead of paying others to do it. This is up from 75 per cent in 2018. In a sign of the times, Coalition voters are now the strongest supporters of rebuilding an active role for government in service delivery. The failure of private contractors to efficiently roll out Covid-19 vaccines will only reinforce this view. Let's not kid ourselves: when lives are on the line, you want someone to take responsibility, not outsource it.

Megalogenis nails this issue, although I wish he had given us more on the central question he poses: can Australia restore faith in good government? His essay dares to dream that Australia can adapt its model of governing and delivering services "to the new consensus for a more active government" and "reconceive the political economy of the nation." I agree that the answer lies in reconnecting with communities, just as Lynelle Briggs found in the aged-care royal commission, and that one part of the answer is a more effective approach by the Commonwealth to partnering with (and funding) state and local governments to deliver services in communities. But I want to suggest the challenge is more profound, for at least two reasons.

First, the *how* is not for the faint-hearted. As Megalogenis writes, "The gaps in the safety net which the coronavirus exploited will become poverty traps in recovery if the government continues to defer to the market." A new approach requires a reorganisation of government and a commitment to regional and community deals involving levels of government alongside business and the community. That's very difficult with anaemic public-sector capability and depleted memory at the national level, especially in social policy. Even if it prefers to fund than to deliver, the Commonwealth will need, and the community will expect, more feet on the ground. Digital delivery helps but is no substitute for interpersonal relationships and knowing what it takes to run things well at neighbourhood level, whether this is in early childhood development, aged care, disability or employment services. Each of these service systems faces acute challenges. Take employment as one example. As of 30 June 2021, there were 1,013,452 Australians on the employment services case load. Around three-quarters have been there for over twelve months. More than a third have been there for more than two years. We have been asleep at the wheel.

Second, this century demands a richer understanding of what a sustainable economy looks like over the long term. Unless we change tack, it will be impossible to disentangle Australia's strategy to exit the pandemic from our future approaches to care, climate change and growth. In each, we see danger signs of the old model: reactive, not proactive, policy development that is based on events, not on evidence and foresight; the government not valuing or nurturing work in the "caring and brain economies" for Australians young and old; and a fossilised approach to boosting economic and social participation in communities in desperate need of new energy and fresh horizons.

Since Megalogenis wrote his essay, the federal government has published its Intergenerational Report, with rosy projections for productivity growth. But at the same time, we have seen a drain of international students and skilled migrants, and a stubborn lack of national planning for carbon transition. Optimistic forecasts are no substitute for an exit strategy.

This future has caught up with us. It demands that Australia change now or be steamrolled. In the run-up to a federal election, the prime minister and Opposition leader need to answer the questions Megalogenis poses. Otherwise, to use a word deployed by the prime minister during the current lockdowns, we will "squander" the natural advantages and opportunities already open to Australia and be on a road from which there is no exit.

Travers McLeod

Rachel Withers

If there was any hope lingering at the end of George Megalogenis's essay that Scott Morrison could take on the lessons of the pandemic and start actively governing; that he might become the ambitious leader we so clearly need him to be, tackling the challenges of the future head-on; or that he could refrain from returning to the "passive and aggressive leader" he was before all this, then the events of winter 2021 have fully extinguished it.

To be fair, Megalogenis doesn't leave us with much optimism – what little there was already trending downwards in the final paragraphs. But like any good Quarterly Essay, *Exit Strategy* ponders a better way forward. "Can Australia restore faith in good government?" Megalogenis asks in the opening chapter. "Will the visceral experience of the pandemic allow us to reconceive the political economy of the nation?" If the 2020 recession does create a reckoning for neoliberalism, as it has in other Western nations, "will Scott Morrison's government have the imagination for the job?" At times, the answer seems to be potentially?

Morrison and his government did show remarkable adaptability, responsiveness and, yes, imagination in the immediate crisis of the pandemic. They listened to experts, put ideology to one side and did what was needed. Morrison may, in fact, have been "the right man to be leading the country in 2020," what with his lack of ideological rigour – Megalogenis clearly shudders, as should we all, at the thought of what might have happened if Tony Abbott and Joe Hockey were still at the helm. Leaders nationwide have been rewarded for Australia's successes with renewed faith in government.

But while Morrison clearly learned a great deal "between the fires and the plague" about crisis management, and while the sidelining of ideology and the elevation of experts was admirable, the prognosis for long-term change is bleak. Morrison, Megalogenis tells us, "has no political interest in talking about the future" and clearly "assumes the old model will reassert itself once the pandemic is over." He remained intentionally passive in many elements of the pandemic. He doesn't seem to be picking up what other leaders are putting down on climate change. He looks mighty ready to exploit once more the electoral divisions he stoked for his "miracle" win in 2019.

The events of June and July have put to rest any promise of a permanently improved politics. In the weeks since this essay was written and published, things have deteriorated dramatically (just as our forward-looking essayist anticipated they might, suggesting that "a third wave of the coronavirus, requiring another extended lockdown, would test the electorate's patience"). Of course, the situation may have improved dramatically by the time you read this – a month is an eternity in politics. But July saw enough poor policy and petty politics to terminate the idea that Morrison could be the man to steer us out of the pandemic and build back for a better future.

The missteps that have dogged the vaccine rollout that was "not a race" have come back to haunt the government, with a major outbreak sending a widely unvaccinated Sydney into an extended lockdown, as well as seeding outbreaks and lockdowns in other states around the country.

But rather than admit fault or take responsibility for his obvious errors, the prime minister has deflected and blamed whoever he can, whether the premiers, global supply chains, hindsight, the virus or even his own health department secretary. We've seen him denigrate the Australian Technical Advisory Group on Immunisation for cautious AstraZeneca advice, which he himself was responsible for incautiously communicating to the public, and we've seen him – intentionally or not – change his government's position on who could access the vaccine without first communicating it to the premiers or chief health officers. We've seen him lie about the rollout timeline, papering over what was promised or even possible, then lie about coming to the rescue with doses that were already coming. We've seen him accuse the Opposition of "playing politics" whenever it poses questions or criticism, after it went easy on him for twelve months. We've not seen him when things go sideways, with the prime minister pulling the sort of disappearing act he surely should have learned by now doesn't appease the public, resurfacing only when polls get really dire.

Throughout this bleak winter crisis, Morrison has not been the collaborative, pragmatic leader who emerged in March 2020. He has been the prime minister Australians recall from the Black Summer bushfires: defensive, thin-skinned, irritable, indignant. Any change we saw in him was temporary, any growth gone; whatever faith in the federal government was rebuilt over the past year is plummeting, with polls again showing a major decline in confidence and trust.

Though the Coalition surprised many in March 2020 by ditching its anti-interventionist principles and introducing JobKeeper and the JobSeeker supplement, this time around it has had to be pressured (or shamed, as the Victorian government put it) into providing every last bit of insubstantial support, even though many people are in the same situation they were in last year. After repeatedly refusing to reintroduce income assistance (so as not to "incentivise" lockdowns), Morrison offered limited, selective, conditional payments to those who had lost work, only to have to boost them, twice, all while refusing to bring back JobKeeper. The age of intervention, to paraphrase Hockey, is over.

This reluctance to provide proper support in the face of lengthy lockdowns should dash hopes that Morrison might have the imagination to join the post-pandemic shift away from neoliberalism.

His denigration of experts does not bode well for the challenges Megalogenis raises around climate change.

The nasty politicking is once again destroying Australia's faith in good government.

It's clear the prime minister will never admit that he was wrong not to bet on several vaccine candidates, to refuse funding for purpose-built quarantine facilities and to push back against lockdowns, even as he rapidly retreats from many of these positions.

But his dismissal of the idea that he could or should have seen any of this coming – accusing people of being critical "in hindsight," admitting only that he failed to "foresee the future" – has highlighted his total lack of foresight or vision, proving once and for all that Morrison is not equipped to face (or even think about) the future.

We all want to believe that our leaders could be better, and Australia's initial success in dealing with the pandemic and its economic shocks was reason to hope that this one actually could. Unfortunately, that hope has proven to be short-lived – not unlike the golden window of summer freedom Australians experienced before the winter of discontent.

Rachel Withers

Andrew Wear

Reading George Megalogenis's eloquent and thoroughly researched essay on Australia's recent political economy, it's hard not to relive the rollercoaster of emotions that accompanied the onset of the pandemic in Australia. His essay recalls the pride in Australia's collective response, the sense of security that came with a system of government that functioned when it needed to, enabling us to get on top of the virus and respond appropriately to the economic challenge. There were the trials and quiet traumas of long lockdowns, accompanied by the guilt that came with the knowledge that what we were suffering did not compare with the devastation experienced in places such as the United States or the United Kingdom. And finally, there is our present bewilderment at Australia's lack of any obvious pathway out of the crisis, even as other nations are opening up.

Megalogenis's central insight – that lessons from past recessions informed our economic response to the pandemic – is an important one. It points to the method we might deploy as we shape our approach to recovery, once we finally figure out how to emerge from the shadow of the pandemic: lessons from past crises have the potential to shape the recovery that remains ahead of us.

Megalogenis shows us that the transfer of insight from the global financial crisis to the present was largely by virtue of the personal experience of Treasury officials. While this demonstrates the value of this type of policy transfer, it also reveals that Australia's approach to learning across time and from other jurisdictions is somewhat ad hoc and perhaps Anglocentric. Other nations, such as Singapore, embed policy transfer deeply into the fabric of their public sectors, regularly sending public servants on learning missions abroad, where they seek to absorb knowledge from the world's best. Australia has room for improvement here.

It must have been challenging for Megalogenis to land a piece like this in the midst of an evolving crisis; the pandemic has yielded a steady supply of plot twists. I am writing this response just as Melbourne enters its sixth lockdown and, with Sydney showing no signs of being able to rein in the virus, it's clear that Australia's response is not quite so textbook as it may have seemed when Megalogenis completed his essay. With the pandemic having a way to run, it's now clear that the depth of the 2020 recession is an inadequate – and overly simplistic – way to assess Australia's economic performance. More important will be where Australia finds itself when the pandemic is over. In May – before Australia's latest Delta-driven wave – the OECD was forecasting that Australia would be back to its pre-pandemic GDP per capita by the first quarter of 2022 (surely now an optimistic assessment), meaning we would have experienced two years of lost growth. That puts us tenth among the G20 countries – mid-pack. While our 2020 recession wasn't as deep, other countries – with higher vaccination rates and more open economies – are recovering faster. As the pandemic has progressed, the importance of the health response to the economy has only become clearer.

While the essay is subtitled "Politics after the Pandemic," its focus is predominantly on politics during – and in the years before – the pandemic. The promise of an exploration of what comes next remains largely unfulfilled. Yet there are enough insights to point us to a method with which to approach the challenges that await. While Australia responded well to the GFC, it squandered the recovery, experiencing a decade of stagnant economic growth, negligible improvements to productivity and median incomes that went backwards. An effective tactical response to the crisis won't be enough if we forgo the opportunity the crisis presents.

Following the Spanish Flu in 1918–19, the United States boomed through the Roaring Twenties, fuelled by new technology and social change. In the 1930s, President Roosevelt's New Deal inspired the confidence that pulled the country out of the Great Depression, with enhanced social security, labour protections and infrastructure investment. Germany and South Korea boomed in the decades after World War II and the Korean War, driven by a determined focus on education and industry policy; both countries pulling themselves out of misery to emerge as among the world's most advanced economies.

What is common to successful recovery from a crisis is a big ambition for what the nation might become, and a preparedness to plan and deliver over the medium to long term. What might such an agenda look like for Australia? Most obviously, fiscal stimulus must flow for as long as it takes to build economic momentum. The opportunity now is to fashion that stimulus into an agenda that fuels long-term economic growth, ideally while tackling legacy challenges at the same time. Megalogenis is right to point to climate change as the obvious candidate here, and there are no shortages of projects that deliver on this dual objective. Large amounts of private-sector capital are poised and ready to be spent on decarbonisation projects. To unlock this potential, it's critical that governments provide policy certainty. This will involve a fast-tracked transformation of energy supply towards renewable sources and investment in infrastructure such as energy storage and transmission. Germany, for example, is investing more than €50 billion of its stimulus on initiatives such as electric vehicle–charging infrastructure and the establishment of a green hydrogen sector, a next-generation export industry that will enable it to store and sell surplus renewable energy. South Korea's "Green New Deal" involves a US$62 billion investment in advanced technology to create jobs – in areas such as renewable electricity, electric vehicles and the circular economy.

The central message that the study of past crises yields, though, is that they do not have to leave a long-term legacy of harm. Places recovering from devastation can create prosperous, exciting futures. People living in New York, Aceh or South Korea now enjoy a quality of life that far exceeds what existed before their crisis. In many instances, such places have not merely recovered, they have gone on to lead the world. It will soon be time – if it's not already – for Australia to craft a similarly suitable ambition for the decade ahead.

Recovery is not guaranteed. History is also strewn with examples of places that failed to recover. They withdrew economic stimulus too early, or held too tight to their pre-crisis world view. As Megalogenis demonstrates, it's important that we approach our future in a considered fashion, learning the lessons of the past. While the Covid-19 pandemic has been the biggest crisis of a generation, our recovery also represents an enormous opportunity.

Andrew Wear

George Megalogenis

In the three weeks between the final edit of my Quarterly Essay on 7 June and its publication on 28 June, a limousine driver in Sydney caught the Delta strain of Covid-19. Among his regular passengers were the crews of international airlines, which placed him on the front line of the NSW quarantine system. His positive test result was announced on 16 June, by which time the virus was already spreading across the city's eastern suburbs. Asked the following day why he had not been vaccinated, NSW premier Gladys Berejiklian explained that there were "literally tens of thousands of people involved in our hotel quarantine system."

"People who are employed directly by police or NSW Health have all been vaccinated, but we also have to appreciate there are new people coming in every day to the system," she told reporters at her daily press briefing. "We've vaccinated all the permanent employees and those in the system [for] a while, but every day there are new people, subcontractors of subcontractors, coming into the system."

It was the type of loophole I might have had in mind when I wrote that "Covid-19 has demonstrated a wicked genius for exploiting the gaps in the old model, most notably in the management of hotel quarantine for returned travellers, and in aged care, where the lines between private and public, and between the federal and state governments, were blurred." But I have to admit that I was surprised by this particular breach. New South Wales had a very clear self-interest in avoiding a repetition of the Victorian experience of 2020, when leaks from its hotel quarantine system unleased a deadly second wave of the virus. Even a cursory check of the NSW system would have identified the flaw. But New South Wales assumed it had nothing to learn from its southern neighbour and rival.

What happened next was even harder to weave into a narrative of public policy competence. The loophole remained in place for a further week and half while NSW Police investigated the Bondi man, and the NSW government resisted pressure to lock down Sydney. Once it was clear that he had broken no laws, and the virus was running ahead, the government turned its mind to catch-up. Private drivers who picked up overseas arrivals were added to the list of essential workers required to wear masks and be vaccinated. On 26 June, the NSW premier announced a lockdown for Greater Sydney, the Blue Mountains, the Central Coast and Wollongong. It was meant to last for just two weeks, but she had already left it too late.

New South Wales had prided itself on managing the virus without closing its economy. Now it was about to learn what Victoria had shown us in 2020: the longer you wait to lock down, the longer the lockdown. Even Scott Morrison, who had framed lockdown as a policy failure when Labor states applied it, now conceded this fundamental point. "The lockdown comes to an end with the lockdown working," the prime minister said in July. "There's not an easy way to bring the cases down, and it's the lockdown that does that work."

At the time of writing, Berejiklian's lockdown has stretched to two months, has been extended to cover the entire state and has no end point in sight. She warned that "September and October will be difficult."

Unlike the Victorian wave, which was largely confined to my hometown of Melbourne, this outbreak has been national in scale and consequence. Up to half the country has been in some form of lockdown as the virus crossed state boundaries. As I write, Melbourne and Canberra are in the middle of what we hope will be four-week lockdowns.

I am mindful that everyone who replied to my essay faced the same challenge that I had in researching and writing it. As Dennis Altman notes, current events "change faster than it takes to produce and circulate an essay."

My essay did not pretend to anticipate subsequent events. Rather, it offered a framework for understanding them. My one big regret is that I underestimated the risk of a double-dip recession in the second half of 2021. I wrote that "a third wave of the coronavirus, requiring another extended lockdown, would test the electorate's patience. Either way, Australia is once again in danger of snatching mediocrity from the jaws of achievement." On reflection, I should have said that it "would test the electorate's patience and could even send the economy back into recession."

Each correspondent has given me something to think about. Jennifer Rayner is correct to say that the power shift to the states predated the pandemic and reflected their collective exasperation with the policy gridlock of the Abbott, Turnbull and Morrison governments. "Looked at this way, what we've seen during the Covid crisis is not an aberration – it's a window into an alternative way to govern the country as we emerge from the pandemic." She notes, for example, that all the states "have signed up to achieve net-zero emissions by 2050."

Richard Denniss was disappointed that I didn't offer a lot more "on possible exit strategies and the political forces that will determine which options are placed on the democratic menu and, ultimately, which dish is selected." I offer my humble apology, but a policy document was beyond the scope of this essay. And the question of which dish is selected from the democratic menu will depend on whether there is a change of government.

I deliberately avoided any speculation on the election once it became clear that the prime minister had abandoned his plan for an early poll in October or November. But I will indulge a short prediction here, to test Dennis Altman's observation that Labor "could easily win government if the five metropolitan areas of Australia voted similarly to Melbourne."

Let's start with the electoral map. The Coalition will enter the next campaign with a notional majority of one – seventy-six seats out of 151 in the House of Representatives – following the redistribution of boundaries to account for population shifts, which added an extra seat for Labor in Melbourne and removed a Liberal seat in Perth. Labor will have sixty-nine seats, while the remaining six are independents or minor parties.

Now the rub for the Opposition. Labor needs a two-party-preferred vote of 51.8 per cent to secure a majority of one. The bar is unusually high because the Coalition has very few ultra-marginal seats on offer to the Opposition. Labor needs a uniform swing of 3.3 per cent to secure the seven seats it requires to govern in its own right. And that's assuming Labor loses no seats of its own to the government. Labor happens to have eight seats on margins of less than 2 per cent.

The government's seven most marginal seats comprise three that the Australian Electoral Commission classify as "inner metropolitan" in Melbourne, Sydney and Perth, one "outer metropolitan" in Adelaide, two "provincial" in Tasmania and Queensland, and one "rural" in Tasmania.

Labor's eight most marginal seats, on the other hand, comprise four provincial seats – two in New South Wales and one each in Victoria and Queensland – another rural seat in New South Wales, as well as two inner metropolitan seats in Brisbane and an outer metropolitan seat in Perth. This map favours the Coalition so long as it can pick off Labor seats outside the cities and force the Opposition to target safer Liberal metropolitan seats.

The Sydney outbreak flips that equation because of its potential to unite voters in the capitals and the regions in common resentment of the Morrison government. Here's how it might play out. Let's assume the Sydney lockdown continues through the spring and into the summer, while other capitals move in and out of lockdown. The national economy will likely contract in both the September and December quarters, meeting the media and political definitions of a recession. That news would be revealed in the national accounts in March next year. Morrison will be reluctant to gamble on a summer election. But nor will he want to wait until the May budget, when the cost of the third wave of the pandemic will be counted in a much larger budget deficit.

It's still too early to say, of course. But the question posed in the subtitle of the essay, "politics after the pandemic," has taken on a different meaning. Of the four scenarios at the next election – the Coalition winning another term in its own right, Labor taking power, or either side forming a minority government – a majority Coalition government is now the least likely.

*

I am grateful that a number of correspondents took time to discuss higher education policy. I'll bounce off their replies, rather than repeat my argument.

Andrew Norton is right when he says that JobKeeper "was never the solution to the problems universities face." The jobs it would have protected would have become unviable at some point, as the economy recovered but international students did not immediately return to their pre-Covid numbers.

Even after the borders eventually reopen in mid-2022, there will be a revenue gap for years to come. "Someone who is not a first-year student in 2021 will not be a second-year student in 2022, and so on. It will take years to rebuild total numbers and fee income."

For Norton, the main concern is the absence of additional assistance for research in 2022, "likely to be the peak year of the Covid crisis in higher education. That was a significant omission in the May 2021 budget." I agree.

One small quibble. Norton seems to think that I "see something wrong with funding private schools." I'm sorry if he read that into my analysis. It isn't my view. My interest was in exploring the political reasons why Coalition governments going back to John Howard tilted the playing field towards private schools, at the expense of universities.

Norton is right that there is blame on both sides for the difficult relationship between the Coalition and the universities, and I share his desire that the next few years will see "fewer avoidable policy and political mistakes than the past few years."

It may depend on Labor's platform. Tanya Plibersek flags an ambitious agenda for universities and TAFE in her reply. If the Morrison government goes into the next election as the underdog, I suspect that the Coalition will swallow its pride and join the bidding war. That was the experience in 2007, when the Howard government tried to counter the electoral appeal of Kevin Rudd's so-called education revolution.

As Michael Wesley points out, the university sector faces further job losses if the Coalition maintains its present course of attrition. "Just as other countries are doubling down on education and research-driven transformations of their economies, Australia will see the atrophy of its knowledge economy."

Travers McLeod reminded me that the Morrison government had more or less declared mission accomplished on the pandemic in May this year, when it wound up the work of the National Covid-19 Coordination Commission. "We have moved past the emergency phase of the Covid-19 response and are now on the path of economic recovery," the prime minister said.

It beggars belief, McLeod writes, that the commission "was told to down tools early," given the Delta strain of the virus was already menacing our region, and Australia was at the bottom of the ladder for vaccinations. Whatever the NCCC was doing, he writes, "it does not appear to have war-gamed different strategies on quarantine hubs or vaccination rollouts, or to have tested various tactics to keep Australia one step ahead of the virus."

Rachel Withers identifies a pattern in Morrison's response to setbacks: the absence of vision. If he admits to any failing at all, it is that he couldn't foresee the future. "We all want to believe that our leaders could be better, and Australia's initial success in dealing with the pandemic and its economic shocks was reason to hope that this one actually could. Unfortunately, that hope has proven to be short-lived – not unlike the golden window of summer freedom Australians experienced before the winter of discontent."

As Andrew Wear notes, that winter could see Australia left behind when the rest of the world is reopening. "While our 2020 recession wasn't as deep, other countries – with higher vaccination rates and more open economies – are recovering faster. As the pandemic has progressed, the importance of the health response to the economy has only become clearer."

At the time of writing, Australia continues to boast one of the lowest death rates from the coronavirus of the thirty-eight nations of the Organisation for Economic Co-operation and Development. The twist is that Australia has also endured the third-toughest restrictions in the OECD over the first eighteen months of the pandemic. To date, the price has been worth paying. But I fear it is exhausting us as a nation.

George Megalogenis

Dennis Altman is a vice-chancellor's fellow at La Trobe University and author of fourteen books, most recently *God Save the Queen: The Strange Persistence of Monarchies*.

Lech Blaine is the author of the memoir *Car Crash*. His writing has appeared in *The Monthly*, *Guardian Australia*, *The Best Australian Essays*, *Griffith Review*, *Kill Your Darlings* and *Meanjin*. He was an inaugural recipient of a *Griffith Review* Queensland Writing Fellowship.

Richard Denniss is chief economist at the Australia Institute. He is the author of *Econobabble*, *Curing Affluenza* and *Dead Right*, and the co-author of *Affluenza*. He writes for *The Monthly*, *The Guardian*, *The Saturday Paper* and *The Australian Financial Review*.

Travers McLeod is the chief executive officer of the Centre for Policy Development, an Australian policy institute.

George Megalogenis's book *The Australian Moment* won the 2013 Prime Minister's Literary Award for Non-fiction and the 2012 Walkley Award for Non-fiction. He is also author of *Faultlines*, *The Longest Decade*, *Australia's Second Chance*, *The Football Solution* and three Quarterly Essays.

Andrew Norton is Professor in the Practice of Higher Education Policy at ANU. From 2011 to 2019, he was higher education program director at the Grattan Institute. In the late 1990s, he was higher education adviser to David Kemp, then the federal minister for education.

Tanya Plibersek is the shadow minister for education, shadow minister for women and the federal member for Sydney.

Jennifer Rayner is the author of *Generation Less* and *Blue Collar Frayed*. She was a senior adviser to ACT chief minister Andrew Barr and former leader of the Opposition Bill Shorten, and currently works as a chief of staff in the ACT government.

Andrew Wear is a senior Australian public servant. His first book, *Solved! How Other Countries Have Cracked the World's Biggest Problems and We Can Too*, was published in 2020. His most recent book is *Recovery: How We Can Create a Better, Brighter Future after a Crisis*.

Michael Wesley is a deputy vice-chancellor and professor of politics at the University of Melbourne. His books include *There Goes the Neighbourhood* and *Restless Continent*.

Rachel Withers is a contributing editor of *The Monthly Today*. Her writing on Australian politics has appeared in *The Saturday Paper*, *Crikey*, *Slate* and *Vox*.